Introduction

Are you tired of trying to get your students to use words other than *very, good,* and *fun* in their writing? Do they repeat the same words over and over again in each sentence they write? Help your students learn new writing skills and "jazz up" their writing using the tools featured in this comprehensive resource.

Use the thought-provoking activities in *Writing Makeovers 5–6* to introduce and review basic writing skills, and use the independent practice pages to reinforce and support these new skills. Each section focuses on an essential writing component and features a coordinating mini-chart with suggested vocabulary or writing strategies.

The activities and practice pages show students how to
- identify nouns and use more descriptive word choices
- use pronouns and their antecedents and be able to clarify them through the use of appositives
- practice using action verbs, verb tenses, and subject-verb agreement
- identify examples of complete sentences, fragments, and compound sentences
- practice identifying and using adjectives
- identify and use a variety of prepositions and phrases
- recognize adverbs and how they are used in written work
- identify the most frequently misspelled words and practice spelling them correctly
- recognize and use correct punctuation

Strong paragraph writing begins with strong sentence writing. Use the step-by-step approach featured in this resource to teach students the key elements of a sentence, and then provide plenty of opportunities for your writers to practice their new skills with activities for the whole class, small groups, pairs, and individuals.

The activities in *Writing Makeovers 5–6* can be selected according to individual needs. Less fluent students will benefit from working with a partner or completing the independent practice pages in a small group.

Using the activities in this resource, students will become more successful writers while gaining knowledge of what it takes to develop better writing skills.

How to Use This Book

The activities in this resource are divided into sections based on the writing concept being taught. Each section includes whole-class, small-group, partner, and independent practice pages. Follow these steps when beginning each section:

Step 1: Practice Pages

Familiarize yourself with the section's opening page, which includes the order in which the activities in the section should be completed and tips for having students complete the independent practice pages.

Step 2: Mini-Chart

Familiarize yourself with the section's mini-chart. Enlarge the chart onto a piece of chart paper, and display it in the classroom. Also, give students a copy of the mini-chart to keep at their desk or in a writing folder.

Step 3: Whole-Class Practice

Have students complete one or more whole-class activities. This will give you a tool for assessing prior knowledge. Have less fluent students repeat activities in a small-group setting.

Step 4: Small-Group Practice

Have students complete one or more small-group activities. Partner up less fluent students with advanced students.

Step 5: Independent Practice

Assign practice pages to each student based on his or her ability level. Review the vocabulary on each page, model how to complete it, and check for understanding before having students work independently. Have less fluent students work with a partner.

Setting the Standards

The standards listed below provide an overview of the skills presented in this resource book.

Reading

Word Analysis, Fluency, and Systematic Vocabulary Development
- Decoding and word recognition
- Vocabulary and concept development

Reading Comprehension
- Comprehension and analysis of grade-level appropriate text
- Expository critique

Literary Response and Analysis
- Structural features of literature
- Literary criticism

Writing

Writing Strategies
- Organization and focus
- Evaluation and revision

Writing Applications
- Genres and their characteristics

Written and Oral English-Language Conventions
- Sentence structure
- Grammar
- Punctuation
- Capitalization
- Spelling

Listening and Speaking Strategies
- Comprehension
- Organization and delivery of oral communication

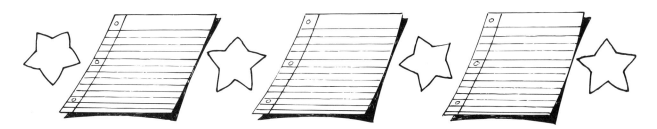

Sentences

This section focuses on using a variety of sentence types and lengths to make writing more interesting. When students know and identify the types of sentences and when they can be joined, their writing becomes more interesting and complex.

Getting Started

• Define

There are **four types of sentences:** declarative, imperative, interrogative, and exclamatory.

Each type of sentence needs a specific type of end punctuation.

The **subject** of the sentence is who or what the sentence is about.

A **simple subject** is a single noun that best describes the subject.

The **predicate** of the sentence is what the subject did or what happened to the subject.

A **simple predicate** is a single verb that best describes what happened.

A **compound subject** has two or more subjects joined together in one sentence.

A **compound predicate** has two or more predicates joined together in one sentence.

A **compound sentence** is made when two simple sentences are joined together using the word *or, and,* or *but.*

• Introduce the Sentences Mini-Chart

Give each student a Sentences Mini-Chart (page 7). Review the concepts, and clarify any concepts with which students may be unfamiliar.

Guided Learning

Have students complete the activities on pages 8–11 before assigning the independent practice pages. Check for understanding by circulating around the classroom during guided learning.

Independent Learning

- **We Had a Grand Time (page 16):** Point out that some fragments give clues.
- **In Your Own Words (page 17):** Encourage students to use details in their sentences. Have them use their mini-chart, if needed.
- **Geronimo, Apache Legend (page 18):** Remind students to find short sentences with repetitive subjects or predicates only.

Wrap-Up

Ask students to write a business letter to their city mayor or city council members about an issue that is of concern to them in their community (e.g., dirty streets, lack of parks, lack of after-school programs). Point out that the format of a business letter is different than a friendly letter. Each student's letter should point out and explain the problem, offer a solution, and persuade the official to agree with his or her point of view.

Sentences Mini-Chart

	declarative	imperative	interrogative	exclamatory
Purpose	makes a statement	gives a command	asks a question	expresses strong emotion
Example	A dark cloud blocked out the sun.	Please tell me about your experience.	What kind of flower is this?	I didn't expect to get any money!
End Mark	**·** period	**·** period	**?** question mark	**!** exclamation point

All complete sentences must have a subject and a predicate.

The **subject** tells who or what the sentence is about. A **simple subject** is a single noun that best describes the subject.

The **predicate** tells what happened to the subject. A **simple predicate** is a single verb that best describes what happened.

Subject	**Predicate**
The white puppy	barked.
Sarah	baked an apple pie.

In some **imperative sentences,** the subject is understood to be "you."
(You)   Please feed my goldfish.
(You)   Put that toy away right now.

A **compound sentence** is made when two simple sentences are joined together using the word *or, and,* or *but.*

Compound subjects
<u>Terry</u> and <u>his little sister</u> ran to the park.

Compound predicates
Yesterday I <u>walked to the pool</u> and <u>swam laps</u>.

Compound sentences
<u>The sign was small</u>, but I <u>could still read it</u>.
<u>The teacher was tired</u>, so <u>I helped her correct papers</u>.
<u>Winter comes</u>, and <u>the snow begins to fall</u>.

Writing Makeovers • 5–6 © 2003 Creative Teaching Press

Objective

Students will identify the subject and predicate in various sentences.

Materials

- Sentences and Fragments reproducible (page 12)
- scissors
- glue
- index cards

Sentences and Fragments

Copy and cut apart the Sentences and Fragments reproducible. Glue each sentence fragment onto an index card. Give each student a prepared index card. Explain to the class that each student has a card with a sentence fragment on it. The fragment is either the subject or the predicate of a sentence. Have each student determine whether his or her card has a subject or a predicate. Then, have a volunteer stand and say *I am looking for a _____ (subject/predicate). Can you complete my sentence?* Have the volunteer read his or her sentence fragment to the class. Invite students to stand if their sentence fragment could make a complete sentence if placed with the volunteer's sentence fragment. Accept all reasonable matches since some may work with more than one fragment. Continue inviting volunteers to read aloud their sentence fragment until all students have had a turn. To extend the activity, invite students to create their own sentence fragments. Have students play the game again with the new sentence fragments.

Types of Sentences

Copy the Sentences Mini-Chart and the Types of Sentences reproducible onto overhead transparencies. Copy a class set of the reproducible. Create six sets of index cards with a period, a question mark, and an exclamation point. (Each set contains three cards.) Display the mini-chart transparency. Review the chart with the class. Discuss hints that will help students identify each type of sentence (e.g., interrogative sentences are looking for an answer, imperative sentences are telling you what to do). Choose six students to be "judges," and give each judge a set of cards. Explain that the judges will hold up the punctuation card that matches the sentence being read and tell what kind of sentence it is. The class must agree or disagree and justify why. If the judges disagree on their answer, invite volunteers to help determine the correct type of sentence. Display the Types of Sentences transparency. Ask a volunteer to read the first sentence. Invite the judges to hold up the correct punctuation card and identify the type of sentence. Ask students to point their thumb up if they agree and down if they disagree. Invite a volunteer to write the type of sentence and add the correct punctuation to the overhead transparency. Continue the activity with the remaining sentences. Remove the transparency, and give each student a Types of Sentences reproducible. Invite students to complete the reproducible independently. Collect the completed papers to check for understanding. *(Sentences 1, 2, 4, 7, 9, 11, and 12 are declarative. Sentences 3 and 14 are exclamatory. Sentences 6 and 10 are imperative. Sentences 5, 8, 13, and 15 are interrogative.)*

Objective

Students will correctly identify types of sentences.

Materials

- Sentences Mini-Chart (page 7)
- Types of Sentences reproducible (page 13)
- overhead projector/ transparencies
- index cards

Combining Sentences

Objectives

Students will

- recognize the repetitive elements in sentences

- combine sentences using conjunctions to remove repetitive words

Materials

✎ Combining Sentences reproducible (page 14)

Write on the board *Jackie got out of bed. Jackie looked out her window to check the weather.* Invite a volunteer to read the sentences. Ask the class if the sentences could be written in a way that relays the same message but is not repetitive. Combine the two sentences into one sentence. Repeat this process with additional sentences. Divide the class into small groups. Give each student a Combining Sentences reproducible. Explain that in Part I group members will read the pairs of sentences and circle the repetitive words. Then, as a group, they will decide how to rewrite the sentences using a conjunction. Point out that students may need to add, delete, or change words so all parts are in agreement, and note that there may be more than one correct answer. Explain that in Part II students are to join the two simple sentences into one sentence. As a group, have students decide if *or, and,* or *but* is the best conjunction for the sentence. Have each group member rewrite the sentence on his or her reproducible. Invite groups to share their answers with the class. To extend the activity, give each student a piece of paper. Invite students to write several simple sentences with repetitive words. Invite students to trade papers with a classmate and rewrite the sentences using a conjunction.

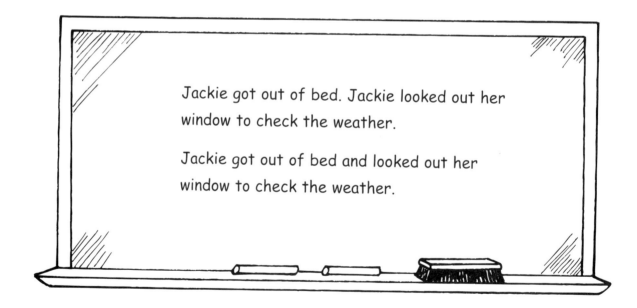

Jackie got out of bed. Jackie looked out her window to check the weather.

Jackie got out of bed and looked out her window to check the weather.

Is That an Interjection or a Direct Address?

Write these three sentences on the board:
Oh, I see what you mean now.
Ouch! I hurt my finger on the glass!
Sarah, could you help me with this window?

Tell students that an interjection is a word or phrase that expresses strong feeling. Read aloud the first two sentences. Point out that these sentences begin with an interjection. Explain that very strong feeling is designated with an exclamation point. Explain that the third sentence begins with a name. Tell students this sentence is an example of a direct address because it shows who the speaker is talking to. Underline *Oh, Ouch,* and *Sarah* in the sentences. Ask students to explain why the interjection or direct address was used in each sentence. Divide the class into pairs, and give each student a What Is It? reproducible. Ask students to underline the interjection or direct address in each sentence and write the underlined word in the correct column at the bottom of their reproducible. Invite partners to share their answers. To extend the activity, invite students to write ten sentences that include an interjection. Invite students to trade papers. Have students circle the interjections on their classmate's paper and then return the paper to the original owner. *(Students should underline* **Dad, Yikes, Justin, Robert, Wow, My, Amy, Gee, Mom, Hooray, Wow,** *and* **Jim.***)*

Objective
Students will recognize interjections and direct address in context.

Materials
✎ What Is It? reproducible (page 15)

Sentences and Fragments

Several unhappy campers	pitched a tent in the pouring rain.
A cool, refreshing waterfall	rushed over rocks to the river below.
A hiker with a golden retriever	followed her dog up the hill.
A fisherman	showed me how to cast my line.
A school of trout	could be seen hiding under the rock ledge.
With a mitt in his hand, the man	walked toward the baseball diamond.
The green canvas tent	was pitched under the big pine tree.
A big black and yellow sign	warned, "Do Not Feed the Bears."
The mosquitoes	sting worse at sundown.
The scent of roasting marshmallows	wafted through the nighttime air.
The glow of the campfire	kept us warm.
The sightseers	saw the most incredible view.
The young hiker	took in the scent of the pine needles.
The campers	washed their dishes in the creek.
Three people with walking sticks	headed off down the trail.
A man and a woman	had a matching pair of jackets.
A large brown bear	rummaged through the trash cans.
A bald eagle	soared on the warm air currents.

Writing Makeovers • 5–6 © 2003 Creative Teaching Press

Name _____   Date _____

Types of Sentences

Directions: Read each sentence. Add the correct punctuation. Write the type of sentence (**declarative**, **exclamatory**, **imperative**, or **interrogative**) on each line.

1. Matter is anything that takes up space   _____

2. The air you breath and the food you eat are all matter   _____

3. Hey, even you are made of matter   _____

4. The three states of matter are solid, liquid, and gas   _____

5. What happens when water is heated or cooled   _____

6. Be careful of hot steam   _____

7. Mass is the amount of matter in an object   _____

8. How much mass do you have   _____

9. Water boils at 212° Fahrenheit   _____

10. Think about it   _____

11. Matter is made up of elements   _____

12. The most dense element is osmium   _____

13. Do you know what a compound is   _____

14. Wow, water is much different than the parts from which it is made   _____

15. Is water a compound   _____

Combining Sentences

Part I

Directions: Read the pair of sentences and circle the repetitive words. Combine the sentences into one sentence using the conjunction **or, and,** or **but.** Write the new sentence on the line.

1. Thorns are a way plants protect themselves. Spines are a way plants protect themselves.

_____

2. The sweet nectar is eaten by ants. The sweet nectar is eaten by bees.

_____

3. Put that notebook on the right side. Put that notebook on the left side.

_____

4. The Venus flytrap eats insects. The pitcher plant eats insects.

_____

5. You depend on plants for food. You depend on plants for shelter.

_____

Part II

Directions: Join the two simple sentences into one sentence with the conjunction **or, and,** or **but.** Write the new sentence on the line.

1. We usually avoid poisonous plants. Some are used for medicine.

_____

2. We get cotton from plants. Some of our food is from plants.

_____

3. Never eat an unfamiliar plant. You could die.

_____

4. The Arctic winds are harsh. Plants remain small.

_____

5. The climate is always frosty. Plants have ways to stay warm.

_____

Writing Makeovers • 5–6 © 2003 Creative Teaching Press

What Is It?

Directions: Underline the interjection or direct address in each sentence. Write each word you underlined in the correct column below.

1. Dad, can you help me build a birdhouse?

2. Yikes! I can't find the screwdriver.

3. Justin, we'll clean up our mess when we are done.

4. Robert, don't use so much glue.

5. Wow, this is easier than I thought it would be.

6. My, the birdhouse turned out really nice.

7. Amy, do you have my baseball bat?

8. Gee, I swore I left it at your house.

9. Mom, maybe it is still in the car.

10. Hooray! I found it.

11. Wow! What a beautiful sunset!

12. Jim, it looks like someone painted it with watercolors.

Shows Feeling	Shows Very Strong Feeling	Shows Who the Speaker Is Talking To
Wow	Yikes!	Dad

We Had a Grand Time

Directions: Read the thank-you letter. Underline the five sentence fragments. Rewrite the letter on a separate piece of paper. Add a subject or predicate to each sentence fragment to make it a complete sentence. Make sure the subjects and predicates agree with the word clues given in the fragments.

July 8, 2002

Dear Aunt Donna and Uncle Vernon,

Want to thank you for inviting us to the beach. Mom and Dad didn't have any plans for Independence Day. After receiving your invitation, my family and I.

Mom said that she enjoyed the peace and quiet. Of course, Dad. My brother loves to play in the waves, even if the water is cold. Like to look for shells to add to my collection.

Now we would like to invite you to our house. This next Labor Day, we. We all look forward to your visit.

Love,

Kelly

In Your Own Words

Directions: Follow the directions below. Use the given information to write each sentence. Be sure to use correct punctuation in each sentence.

1. Write a declarative sentence about baseball.

   _____

2. Write an interrogative sentence about sea stars.

   _____

3. Write an exclamatory sentence about parasailing.

   _____

4. Write an imperative sentence about video games.

   _____

5. Write an interrogative sentence about a new movie. Include an interjection.

   _____

6. Write a declarative sentence about washing hands.

   _____

7. Write an exclamatory sentence about a recent school event. Include an interjection.

   _____

8. Write a declarative sentence about babysitting.

   _____

9. Write an imperative sentence about your homework.

   _____

10. Write an interrogative sentence about a pet.

   _____

Writing Makeovers • 5–6 © 2003 Creative Teaching Press

Name _____   Date _____

Geronimo, Apache Legend

Directions: Read the passage. Underline the four **pairs** of sentences with repetitive words. Use a conjunction to combine the underlined sentences to make a complex sentence. Rewrite the revised sentences on a separate piece of paper.

Geronimo was born in 1829. Geronimo lived in the mountains of southern Arizona. At the time of his birth, no problems appeared between the Apache and the white immigrants. There were no railroads. There were very few wagon trains. However, soon Apache land would be claimed by the United States of America. The Apache could give in to the United States' demands or could die fighting.

Following the Mexican War, the United States gained the state of Texas. The United States gained the land that is now Arizona, Colorado, New Mexico, and California. The Americans promised Mexico that they would control the Apache raids on Mexican towns. The Apache did not understand this. The raids were something that had been a part of their culture for centuries.

Geronimo's family was massacred in an attack by Mexican troops. Geronimo's whole village was massacred in an attack by Mexican troops. Geronimo now wanted revenge. He convinced other warriors to fight with him. This band of Apache had many successful raids on Mexican settlements. Soon they found themselves up against U.S. troops. Geronimo felt he could trust no one but his own.

Geronimo was finally forced to surrender on September 4, 1886. This proud Apache was moved from reservation to reservation. He spent his later years touring fairs and expositions. His status as a fierce warrior had made him an American legend.

Writing Makeovers • 5–6 © 2003 Creative Teaching Press

Nouns, Pronouns, and Appositives

Students will begin to understand that certain nouns add more description to their writing. Students will learn that appositives are phrases that help define a noun in a sentence, but that they should be used in moderation so they do not become overused and repetitive themselves.

Getting Started

- **Define**

    A **noun** is a person, place, thing, or idea. Nouns can be common or proper.

    A **pronoun** is a word that takes the place of a noun. Pronouns fit into the following categories: **subject pronouns, object pronouns, possessive pronouns,** and **indefinite pronouns.**

    An **appositive** is a word or phrase that follows a noun and gives more details about the noun. It is set apart with commas.

- **Introduce the Nouns, Pronouns, and Appositives Mini-Chart**

    Give each student a Nouns, Pronouns, and Appositives Mini-Chart (page 20). Review the word lists, and clarify the meaning of any words with which students may be unfamiliar.

Guided Learning

Have students complete the activities on pages 21—24 before assigning the independent practice pages. Check for understanding by circulating around the classroom during guided learning.

Independent Learning

- **Searching for Nouns and Pronouns (page 27):** Review with students the difference between proper nouns, common nouns, and pronouns.
- **Letter to Aunt Kathy (page 28):** To extend the activity, invite students to write a letter to someone they know and include at least five pronouns.
- **Hard Traveling on the Oregon Trail (page 29):** Answers may vary. Students may replace the "worn out" words with *women, Conestoga wagon* or *covered wagon, men, stallion, pioneer* or *settler, Conestoga wagon* or *covered wagon, pushcart, possessions, settlements, possessions, mules, children, pack, supplies, settlers* or *pioneers,* and *Oregon Territory.*
- **Tale of Two States (page 30):** Students should select, in order, *our 31st state, California's state capital, an award-winning author, the Gold Rush, Los Angeles, New York, Albany, our 32nd U.S. president, a symbol of freedom,* and *the largest city in the United States.*
- **In Other Words: Women (page 31):** Discuss with the class the importance of using more descriptive words in writing.

Wrap-Up

Have students write about the members of their family. Tell students to give details about each family member's appearance and personality, where he or she likes to go, and the things he or she likes to do.

Nouns, Pronouns, and Appositives Mini-Chart

A **common noun** is a person, place, thing, or idea. A **proper noun** is the specific name of a noun and it is capitalized.

People	Places	Things	Ideas
man	mountain	car	togetherness
adolescent	hill	sedan	unity
father	knoll	convertible	merger
citizen	peak	vehicle	consolidation
Ralph	Mount Fuji	Corvette	honesty

A **pronoun** is a word that takes the place of a noun.

Subject Pronouns	Object Pronouns	Possessive Pronouns
he	him	his
she	her	her/hers
I	me	my/mine
they	them	their/theirs
we	us	our/ours
who	whom	whose
you	you	your/yours
it	it	its

An **indefinite pronoun** does not refer to a particular person, place, or thing.

everybody	anybody	somebody	nobody	each	most
everyone	anyone	someone	no one	all	some
everything	anything	something	nothing	both	many

An **appositive** is a word or phrase that follows a noun and gives more details about the noun.

For example
* Mount Whitney, <u>the highest mountain in California,</u> is a favorite vacation spot.
* My oldest sister, <u>Sarah,</u> teaches swimming on the weekend.

Writing Makeovers • 5–6 © 2003 Creative Teaching Press

Take My Place

Copy the Nouns, Pronouns, and Appositives Mini-Chart onto a piece of chart paper. Copy the Take My Place reproducible onto an overhead transparency, and copy a class set of the reproducible. Display the prepared chart. Point out to the class the subject and object pronouns on the mini-chart. Explain that a subject pronoun appears in the subject of the sentence and is who or what the sentence is about. Explain that an object pronoun receives the action of the sentence and is part of the predicate. Display the Take My Place transparency. Ask a volunteer to read aloud the first two sentences. Have students identify the repetitive nouns that appear in the two sentences. Invite volunteers to edit the sentences by crossing out the nouns that can be replaced with a pronoun. Point out that the first time the noun appears it should not be replaced. Explain that this is because a pronoun needs to refer to a specific noun. Give each student a Take My Place reproducible. Explain to the class that an antecedent is the noun to which the pronoun refers. Have students rewrite the sentences with the new pronoun choices. Ask them to draw arrows that connect the pronoun with its antecedent. Circulate around the classroom to check for understanding.

Objective

Students will identify subject and object pronouns and their antecedents in sentences.

Materials

- Nouns, Pronouns, and Appositives Mini-Chart (page 20)
- Take My Place reproducible (page 25)
- chart paper
- overhead projector/ transparency

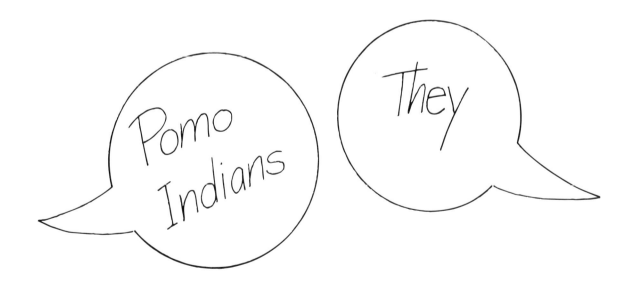

A Noun By Any Other Name

Objective

Students will recognize that the choice of nouns affects the readers' mental image of the text.

Materials

- A Noun By Any Other Name reproducible (page 26)
- overhead projector/transparency
- scratch paper

Copy the A Noun By Any Other Name reproducible onto an overhead transparency. Divide the class into small groups. Give each group a piece of scratch paper, and assign each group one of the following words from the transparency: *flower, plant, woman, mammal, bird, shoes, water, building,* and *car.* Explain to the class that each group will have 3 minutes to list on their scratch paper as many nouns as they can that are more descriptive replacements for their assigned word. After the 3 minutes, display the transparency, and invite groups to share their word list. Record student responses in the appropriate box on the transparency. Discuss how the choice of different nouns affects the mental picture formed by a reader. Then, read each sentence at the bottom of the transparency, and invite volunteers to underline the nouns in the sentences and add the applicable nouns to the appropriate box above.

Pronoun Proclamations

Write on separate index cards the possessive and indefinite pronouns from the Nouns, Pronouns, and Appositives Mini-Chart. Display the word cards one at a time to the class. Ask for volunteers to use each word in a sentence and share if it is a possessive or an indefinite pronoun. For example, a student might say **Nothing** *belongs on the shelf* or *Mrs. Thomas didn't know* **anybody** *at the party*. Divide the class into small groups. Give each group a piece of writing paper. Shuffle the word cards, and pass out an equal number of cards to each group. Ask groups to create a story that includes all the words on their cards. Explain that every sentence must include one of the pronouns and be connected by a common story line. Have groups share their story with the class and display the matching word card each time they read one of their pronouns.

Objective

Students will recognize possessive and indefinite pronouns and use them correctly in sentences.

Materials

- Nouns, Pronouns, and Appositives Mini-Chart (page 20)
- index cards
- writing paper

Adding Meaning with Appositives

Objective

Students will recognize nouns and their appositives and use them correctly in writing.

Materials

✑ writing paper

Select a recent social studies or science topic that your class has studied. Have students brainstorm a list of nouns related to the topic. Record student responses on the board. Explain that an appositive is a word or a group of words that tells more about the noun of the sentence. Explain that an appositive directly follows the noun and is set off between commas. Write the following sentences on the board:

The United States, **a large country,** *spans from one ocean to another. The microscope,* **an instrument for magnification,** *should be used with care.*

Read aloud the sentences, and point out the appositives. Invite volunteers to select a noun from the brainstormed list and use it in a sentence, adding appositives. Divide the class into pairs. Give each pair a piece of writing paper. Tell students to use each noun from the list in a sentence and add an appositive to help define the noun. Remind students to use in their sentences details that they have learned in their studies. Have partners underline the appositives and make sure they have included commas in each sentence.

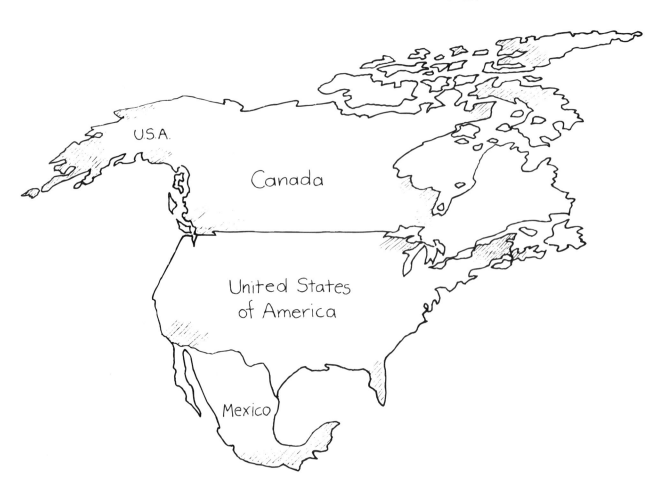

Take My Place

Directions: In each set of sentences, identify the repetitive noun that can be replaced with a pronoun and draw an X over it. Rewrite the sentences with appropriate pronouns. Draw an arrow that connects the pronoun with its antecedent. Remember: The first noun is not repetitive and should not be replaced with a pronoun.

1. The Pomo Indians wove elaborate baskets. The Pomo Indians used the reeds from the lakes to create the baskets.

   _____

   _____

2. A Shoshone tribesman used a horse for hunting. A Shoshone tribesman traded his horse with his neighbors to the east, the Nez Percé and the Crow.

   _____

   _____

3. Chief Joseph was a famous Nez Percé chief. The land of his ancestors was important to Chief Joseph.

   _____

   _____

4. In the northwest, a Haida woman would clean the fish. A Haida woman would lay the fish on racks to dry.

   _____

   _____

5. My classmates and I study Native Americans to understand other cultures. My classmates and I find these customs and ways of life interesting.

   _____

   _____

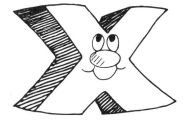

A Noun By Any Other Name

flower	plant	woman
mammal	bird	shoes
water	building	car

1. Several red roses bloomed beside the old wooden shack at the edge of the pond.

2. My dad's black sedan needed to be washed, so my sister volunteered to wash it.

3. In the morning, Renee watched a robin search for insects under the lilac.

4. The grasses that grow by the ocean are home to sandpipers and mice.

5. A tall lady walked by in a new pair of red pumps.

6. Taylor's hiking boots were wet from the walk across the stream by the old oak tree.

Searching for Nouns and Pronouns

Directions: Underline the common noun, proper noun, and/or pronoun in each sentence. See if you can find 32 different nouns. Write each underlined word in the proper column in the chart below. Remember that there may be more than one noun or pronoun in a sentence.

1. The ear is a complex part of your body.

2. The outer ear is shaped like a funnel and it contains the eardrum.

3. The hammer, the anvil, and the stirrup are three tiny bones.

4. As you listen to "The Star-Spangled Banner," they pass the vibrations on to the cochlea.

5. Alexander Graham Bell invented many things to help people hear well.

6. His experiments led to the invention of the telephone.

7. My sister, Teresa, can hear really high and low sounds.

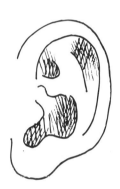

8. I can hear someone whistling across the meadow.

9. That loud voice I hear is hers.

10. Everyone should be careful around loud noises.

Common Nouns	Proper Nouns	Pronouns

Letter to Aunt Kathy

Directions: Read the letter. Replace each underlined noun with a pronoun. Reread the letter to make sure the pronouns you chose convey who is speaking and to what or whom they are referring.

August 18, 2002

Dear Aunt Kathy,

Did <u>Aunt Kathy</u> have a good birthday? Mom said that <u>Aunt Kathy</u> went to Yosemite to celebrate. <u>Mom</u> said that you told her <u>Yosemite</u> was very crowded at this time of year. <u>The person writing this letter</u> went to the waterpark yesterday. Sarah, Mario, and Thomas went, too. <u>Sarah, Mario, and Thomas</u> have a season pass and can go whenever their parents take <u>Sarah, Mario, and Thomas</u>. Sarah won't be at my school next year. Sarah's dad was transferred to Chicago and <u>Sarah and her dad</u> will be moving in September. Sarah's dad is already living in Chicago. Did you ever meet <u>Sarah's dad</u>? Mom says hello. Mom wants you to come visit in the fall. Please write <u>the person writing this letter</u> back soon.

Love,

Jeanette

Name _____   Date _____

Hard Traveling on the Oregon Trail

Directions: Read the paragraph. The underlined words are "worn-out" nouns. Use the word bank to help you select a more appropriate noun for each underlined word. Write the selected noun above the appropriate underlined noun. Reread the paragraph with the new nouns to make sure it makes sense.

Word Bank

women	Oregon Territory	men	pushcart	settler(s)	pioneer(s)	possessions
settlements	Conestoga wagon	mules	supplies	pack	children	belongings
stallion	covered wagon					

When someone mentions the Oregon Trail, do you picture in your mind <u>people</u> sitting in a <u>thing</u> and <u>people</u> riding on the back of a(n) <u>animal</u>? This was not always the way it was. Not every <u>person</u> traveled in a <u>thing</u>. Many people used a wooden <u>thing</u>, like a large wheelbarrow, to pull or push their <u>things</u> to the new <u>place</u> in Oregon. Imagine pushing all of your <u>things</u> across the country in a wheelbarrow! Others used <u>animals</u> because they could carry large loads. Many pioneers, even the youngest <u>people</u>, just walked with a <u>thing</u> on their back. This was the most they could afford. In later years, wealthy families traveled in fancy vehicles that also carried a cook, a real stove, and boxes of needed <u>things</u>. No matter rich or poor, these determined <u>persons</u> wanted more than anything to start over in the <u>place</u>.

Nouns, Pronouns, and Appositives   29

Tale of Two States

Directions: Read each sentence. Write on each line an appositive from the word bank that helps define the noun that comes before it. Look for clues in the sentence to help you choose the correct appositive.

Word Bank

Albany	the largest city in the United States	our 31st state
the Gold Rush	an award-winning author	Los Angeles
New York	our 32nd U.S. president	
a symbol of freedom	California's state capital	

1. California, _____, was admitted to the union in 1850.

2. Sacramento, _____, is located in the northern part of the state.

3. John Steinbeck, _____, wrote The Grapes of Wrath about the poor migrant workers in California.

4. An event in 1848, _____, brought many gold miners to California.

5. The largest city in California, _____, has over 3 million people.

6. Our 11th state, _____, became part of the United States in 1788.

7. New York's state capital, _____, is north of New York City.

8. Franklin Delano Roosevelt, _____, was born in New York.

9. The Statue of Liberty, _____, holds her torch high above New York Harbor.

10. New York City, _____, has over 8 million people living there.

Writing Makeovers • 5–6 © 2003 Creative Teaching Press

Name _____   Date _____

In Other Words: Women

Directions: The word bank contains more descriptive nouns to replace the missing noun **woman** in each sentence. Read each sentence carefully. Select the most appropriate noun from the word bank to complete each sentence. Use each word only once.

Word Bank

customer	saleswoman	mother	aunt
teacher	grandmother	doctor	congresswoman
gymnast	actress	sister	scientist

1. The _____ waited impatiently as the others voted on her new law.

2. Because the scene had to be reshot, the _____ could not rest for another hour.

3. My _____ taught me how to knit; she and my mother had learned from their mother.

4. The new _____ appeared nervous, but as she turned to face the class, she had a broad smile on her face.

5. The baby cooed as the young _____ held him in her arms.

6. The crowd cheered when the _____ finished her routine with a perfect score.

7. Another patient was waiting when the _____ opened her door.

8. The new _____ sold more clothes this month than any other employee.

9. The _____counted out dollar bills in order to pay for her purchase.

10. I only see my _____ once a month, but she teaches me how to cook her favorite recipes.

11. My _____ is only three years older than I am, but she acts like she knows everything.

12. The _____ put on her lab coat before she began to mix the chemicals for the experiment.

# Verbs

This section focuses on different types of verbs, including action verbs, linking verbs, and state of being verbs. Students begin by identifying action verbs and finding more vivid replacements. Students determine correct verb tenses and choose proper linking verbs that agree with the subject. They replace overused verbs with verbs that have a more precise meaning.

Getting Started

• **Define**

A **verb** is a word that tells what a noun does.

An **action verb** is a word that expresses an action.

A **verb phrase** is a main verb and all of its helping verbs.

A **helping verb** helps the main verb show action or make a statement.

A **direct object** is a noun or pronoun in the predicate that receives the action of a verb.

An **indirect object** is a noun or pronoun in the predicate that answers the question *to whom? for whom? to what?* or *for what?* following an action verb.

A **linking verb** links the subject of a sentence to a noun or an adjective in the predicate.

Verb tenses help tell when an action is taking place: present, past, or future.

• **Introduce the Verbs Mini-Chart**

Give each student a Verbs Mini-Chart (page 33). Review the word lists, and clarify the meaning of any words with which students may be unfamiliar.

Guided Learning

Have students complete the activities on pages 34–37 before assigning the independent practice pages. Check for understanding by circulating around the classroom during guided learning.

Independent Learning

• **A Bit of a Fright (page 42):** Students should write, in order, *dared, enter, teased, accepted, forget, peered, thought, heard, caught, shivered, creeping,* and *giggled.*

• **Making Paper Money (page 43):** Point out that the mini-chart has a list of linking and helping verbs. Remind students of the definition of a linking verb.

• **Said, Went, and Have (page 44):** Review verb tenses before students complete this activity. Some irregular verbs, such as *go* and *went* or *run* and *ran,* will need to be changed before students understand how they can replace *said, went,* and *have.*

• **Bette Nesmith Graham (page 45):** Discuss the use and meaning of the synonyms for *ask* and *make* before students complete this activity.

Wrap-Up

Have students write a paragraph that explains how to do something. Tell them to include vivid verbs that help their audience picture exactly what it is that they are supposed to do.

Verbs Mini-Chart

A **verb** is a word that tells what a noun does.

The "worn-out" verbs in the top row can be replaced with one of the more vivid verb choices shown below.

said	went	made	have	ask
announced	marched	built	accept	demand
asked	proceeded	caused	borrow	examine
exclaimed	sauntered	completed	comprise	inquire
proclaimed	strolled	created	contain	ponder
screamed	swayed	earned	hold	pose
stated	traveled	fashioned	include	query
uttered	trekked	finished	own	request
whispered	walked	prepared	possess	solicit

A **main verb** and a **helping verb** go together. They make up a **verb phrase.** These helping verbs will start a verb phrase. (Note: Some verbs, such as *am, are, is, was,* and *were,* fit in more than one category.)

am	be	do	have	my	was
are	being	does	has	might	were
is	been	did	had	must	will
	can			shall	would
	could			should	

A **linking verb** does not show action. A linking verb links the subject to a noun or an adjective in the predicate. These are linking verbs if they are followed by an adjective or a noun.

am	be	become	look	appear	were
are	being	smell	stay	feel	was
is	seem	taste	was		

Verb tenses give clues to when an action happened. Use the proper verb tense to match when something occurred.

past	present	future
caught	catch	will catch
disagreed	disagree	will disagree
found	find	will find
revolved	revolve	will revolve
wrote	write	will write

Objectives

Students will

• identify and recognize action verbs

• distinguish between physical actions and mental actions

Materials

✇ Thoughts by a Full Moon reproducible (page 38)

✇ overhead projector/transparency

✇ chart paper

Ready, Set, Action!

Copy the Thoughts by a Full Moon reproducible onto an overhead transparency. Draw two columns on a piece of chart paper. Label the first column *Physical Action Verbs* and the second column *Mental Action Verbs*. Display the prepared chart. Explain to the class that an action verb tells what the subject is doing. Explain that this action can be something physical such as walking or mental such as thinking. Display the transparency. Have students read aloud the poem. Then, ask for volunteers to explain what the poem means. Ask students to name the action verbs in the poem and consider whether each verb describes a physical action or a mental action. Record each verb in the appropriate column on the chart paper. After discussing the action verbs from the poem, ask students to brainstorm more physical and mental actions that can be added to the chart. To extend the activity, have students determine if the verbs on the chart are past, present, or future tense. *(Students should find the physical verbs **rest, gazing, shines, illuminating, see, come, awaits, sigh, smile, change,** and **revolve.** They should find the mental verbs **think, wonder, know, accepting,** and **forget.**)*

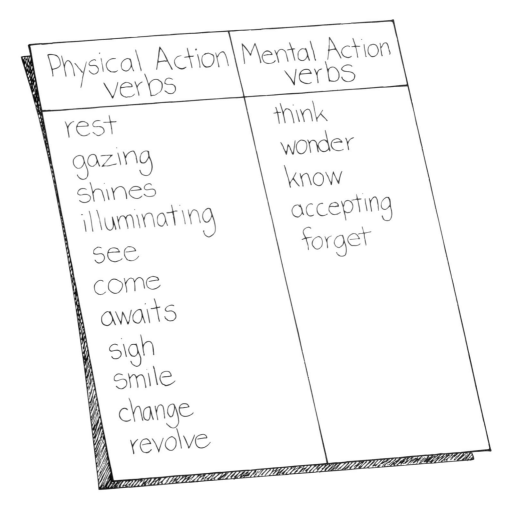

Physical Action Verbs	Mental Action Verbs
rest	think
gazing	wonder
shines	know
illuminating	accepting
see	forget
come	
awaits	
sigh	
smile	
change	
revolve	

Yesterday, Today, and Tomorrow

Copy the Yesterday, Today, and Tomorrow reproducible onto an overhead transparency, and display it. Explain that the transparency shows a page out of a student's daily planner. Ask students to silently read the entries. Ask a volunteer to state a complete sentence that uses the information from the planner and a proper verb tense. For example, a student might say *Karla* **gets** *her allowance today*. Record the student's response on the board. Underline the verb as the student identifies it. Explain that vivid verbs add more interesting details to sentences. Have the student repeat the sentence. Invite another volunteer to use a more vivid verb, if needed, to give the sentence more detail. For example, *Karla will* **receive** *her allowance today*. Point out that the verb has changed, but ask students to identify how the verb choice has given more details about Karla and her emotions. Repeat the activity with additional sentences. Have students select eight entries from the transparency and rewrite them with more vivid verbs. Give students a thesaurus, if needed. Invite volunteers to share one of their revised sentences with the class.

Objective

Students will use proper verb tenses and replace worn-out verbs.

Materials

- Yesterday, Today, and Tomorrow reproducible (page 39)
- overhead projector/ transparency
- thesauruses

Verb Phrases in Action

Objectives

Students will

- add the correct pronouns to the verb phrases and then expand the sentences
- identify nouns and pronouns in sentences

Materials

- Verb Phrases in Action reproducible (page 40)
- writing paper

Give each student a Verb Phrases in Action reproducible. Ask volunteers to read aloud the verb phrases on the reproducible. Clarify any unfamiliar verbs. Write *I, You, We, They, He, She,* and *It* on the board. Have volunteers combine one of the listed pronouns with a verb phrase so that the pronoun agrees with the helping verb. For example, for the first phrase, *am irritated,* a student could say *I am irritated.* Point out that because the first phrase contains the helping verb *am,* only *I* can be paired with it. Divide the class into small groups. Give each group a piece of writing paper. Assign each group a portion of the verb phrases, and ask groups to write their verb phrases on their paper. Have groups add a pronoun to each phrase and expand it into a sentence. For example, *I am irritated by my new wool sweater.* Have students underline all the pronouns. Encourage students to circle all additional nouns. Encourage groups to link their sentences together with some common theme. Invite groups to act out their sentences for the class.

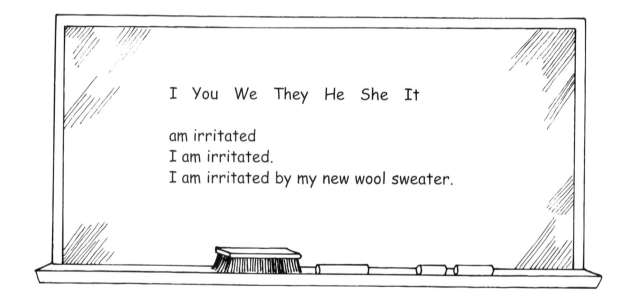

Linking Words Together

Write on the board *I am tired* and *I am a pianist*. Underline the linking verb *am* in each sentence. Explain to the class that *am* is a linking verb because it does not show action, but links the subject with either another noun or an adjective. In the sentence *I am tired*, *I* is the subject and *tired* is an adjective that describes the subject. *Am* links *I* and *tired*. In the sentence *I am a pianist*, *I* is the subject and *pianist* is a noun. *Am* links *I* and *pianist*. Point out that some of these linking verbs are also action verbs. Remind students that a linking verb does not express action. It expresses a state of being. For example, in the sentence *I smell the flower*, *smell* expresses an action. However, in the sentence *The flower smells wonderful*, *smells* links *flower* to the adjective *wonderful*. It is not an action done by the flower. Divide the class into pairs. Give each pair a Linking Words Together reproducible. Have partners read each sentence, underline the linking verb, and circle the words it links together. *(Students should identify these words: 1.* **am** *links* **I** *and* **guard** *2.* **are** *links* **friends** *and* **late** *3.* **is** *links* **school** *and* **building** *4.* **must be** *links* **We** *and* **careful** *5.* **stay** *links* **students** *and* **busy** *6.* **seems** *links* **day** *and* **shorter** *7.* **became** *links* **sky** *and* **dark** *8.* **looks** *links* **weather** *and* **stormy** *9.* **was** *links* **There** *and* **chance** *10.* **were** *links* **People** *and* **happy** *11.* **are being** *links* **friends, I,** *and* **silly** *12.* **tastes** *links* **it** *and* **sweet** *13.* **is** *links* **store** *and* **busy** *14.* **smells** *links* **grass** *and* **sweet** *15.* **appeared** *links* **sky** *and* **clear.)*

Objectives

Students will
- identify linking verbs in sentences
- identify the nouns and adjectives that are connected by linking verbs

Materials

✎ Linking Words Together reproducible (page 41)

Thoughts by a Full Moon

I rest upon a rock gazing down
over a silvery lake.
A full moon shines above my head
illuminating what I see.
I think about the day to come
and wonder what awaits me

I know not what
And so …

I sigh and smile to myself
accepting what I cannot change.
But for the moment I forget
the world does not revolve around me.

—Pamela Jennett

Yesterday, Today, and Tomorrow

Karla keeps a daily planner. Here are her entries for the first three days of the week.

Monday

Bicycle with Steve to school

Lunch in auditorium

Science club meeting

Afternoon soccer practice

Tuesday

Ride with Mom to school

Bring paper bag lunch

Lunchtime choir practice

Uniform ready at dry cleaners

Allowance Day!

Wednesday

Bicycle to school

Biology report due

Band practice at 3:00

One hour clarinet practice

Writing Makeovers • 5–6 © 2003 Creative Teaching Press

Verb Phrases in Action

1 am irritated	**2** are quoting	**3** is squandering	**4** could conduct
5 are purchasing	**6** can gloat	**7** may magnify	**8** must halt
9 was expired	**10** might comprehend	**11** has resisted	**12** did guarantee
13 can loiter	**14** should forgive	**15** had hidden	**16** have commented
17 were mispronouncing	**18** must have squabbled	**19** am operating	**20** will be parachuting
21 may compensate	**22** have compared	**23** could be frightened	**24** do oblige
25 shall obey	**26** has preserved	**27** does not argue	**28** should have preferred
29 should refuse	**30** was elected	**31** had fainted	**32** could duplicate
33 is capturing	**34** were not strolling	**35** shall overrule	**36** might be scanning
37 has not been purified	**38** have sipped	**39** might skid	**40** is colliding

Writing Makeovers • 5–6 © 2003 Creative Teaching Press

Linking Words Together

Directions: Read each sentence. Underline the linking verb. Circle the words it links together. The first one has been done for you.

1. In the morning, (I) <u>am</u> a crossing (guard) at the corner.

2. My friends are late for school today.

3. My school is a brick building three blocks away.

4. We must be careful as we cross the street.

5. The students stay busy with their assignments.

6. The day seems shorter than it usually does.

7. The sky became dark as the heavy clouds moved in.

8. The weather looks stormy to me.

9. There was a chance we would get rain.

10. People were happy to move inside.

11. My friends and I are being silly as we stop at the store.

12. I buy a soda and it tastes too sweet.

13. The store is busy with other customers.

14. Outside, the fresh cut grass smells sweet to me.

15. Meanwhile, the sky appeared clear.

A Bit of a Fright

Directions: Circle all the verbs in the word bank. Use the verbs to fill in the blanks to complete the story.

Word Bank

caught	giggled	creeping	three	forget
nervously	shivered	goblin	Megan	sister
okay	peered	heard	accepted	teased
dark	thought	movement	enter	dared

An old abandoned house stood at the end of the street. Megan _____ her

friend Jimmy that he would not _____ the old house. "I'm sure it is haunted," she

_____.

Jimmy _____ the dare, and he challenged, "I'll go if you go as well."

"Don't _____ me! I want to go, too," cried Shannon, Megan's younger sister.

The three children _____ through the door and then stepped inside. The

house looked okay. It wasn't as dark as they _____ it would be.

Suddenly, they _____ light footsteps, step-step-stepping, coming closer

and closer. A movement from the next room _____ their eye. Shannon

_____.

"Why, it's only a cat _____ across the floorboards!" exclaimed Megan. All

three children _____ nervously as they scurried back out the front door.

Writing Makeovers • 5–6 © 2003 Creative Teaching Press

Making Paper Money

Directions: Read the story and circle the 17 action verbs. Draw a box around the nine helping verbs. Underline the four linking verbs.

The Chinese were the first culture to use paper money. The Chinese had perfected the art of printing with wood blocks. They printed detailed images onto cloth or paper. Chinese paper was made from the fibers of mulberry bark, bamboo shoots, and cloth. These fibers softened in a water bath. The fibers were mashed. They became a pulp. Thin layers of pulp were laid over a wide screen of mesh. The pulp dried on these screens. After it dried, the pulp was removed from the screens. It was trimmed and pressed so it was as smooth as possible. The pulp was now sheets of paper! A wood block had been carved with a design. This design represented the Chinese paper currency. The paper was pressed against the wood block. The ink on the wood block marked the paper with the design. Then the money could be spent.

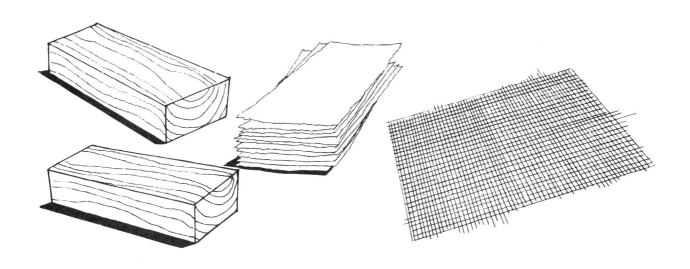

Said, Went, and Have

Directions: The words **said, went,** and **have** are overused in writing. Circle these verbs in the sentences. Then, replace these overused words with more appropriate verbs. Use your mini-chart for suggestions. Use each verb only once. Write a new verb next to each sentence and in the correct column below.

1. Kelly and Rick went down the street. _____

2. "Can I have a ten-dollar bill?" asked Kelly. _____

3. They went through a gate under a large sign that announced, "Circus Today."

   _____

4. Rick said, "Do we have enough money to get in?" _____

5. The woman in the ticket booth said, "You are holding plenty of money." _____

6. The children went past a large tent as a man said, "Come on inside." _____

   _____

7. "Maybe we should see this," said Kelly. _____

8. Three horses went in a circle as acrobats jumped from back to back. _____

9. "Hey, our ticket price has a free soda," said Rick. _____

   _____

10. The children exited from the tent and went home. _____

said	went	have

Writing Makeovers • 5–6 © 2003 Creative Teaching Press

Bette Nesmith Graham

Directions: The words **asked** and **make (made)** are overused in the story. Read the story and circle these overused verbs. Replace as many of these verbs as you can with synonyms from your mini-chart or a thesaurus to help you make the story more interesting. Write the new verbs above the circled verbs. Reread the story to check that your new verbs make sense in context.

Bette Nesmith Graham was a young single mother in the 1950s. As a secretary in a typing pool, she made very little money. Then she asked about a job as an executive secretary for a large bank. This was a good job and she would make more money. Bette was hired and right away she wanted to make a good impression. The bank used the new electric typewriters, which Bette had not used before. However, Bette asked a lot of questions and was a quick learner. She found the new typewriters much easier to use, except for one problem. As she was typing, Bette would occasionally make a mistake. She tried to erase the mistake. The more she erased, the more of a mess the ink made. "How can I fix my mistakes so they aren't so smudgy?" Bette asked. Then Bette remembered that artists do not erase their mistakes, they paint over them!

Bette made a "mistake-fixer" from white tempera paint. She could paint right over the top of a mistake and no one could tell! Soon, other secretaries asked Bette to share her secret. She made a container from a bottle she had at home and labeled it "Mistake Out." Before too long, an office supply dealer asked, "Why don't you market 'Mistake Out'?" It took a lot of time and effort, but Bette did just that. Eventually Bette made Liquid Paper® and made a lot of money. Bette Nesmith Graham made it a lot easier for the rest of us to fix our mistakes!

Adjectives and Prepositions

This section focuses on the use of adjectives and prepositions to develop meaning in writing. Students will learn that when they properly use adjectives, the subject and object of the sentence are easier for the reader to picture. Prepositional phrases function as adjectives and add complexity as well.

Getting Started

- **Define**

    An **adjective** is a word that describes a noun or pronoun. It tells *what kind, how many,* or *which one.*

    When comparing nouns in a sentence, the **comparative form** of an adjective is used. Use an adjective with *-er* or *more* when comparing two nouns. Use a **superlative adjective** with *-est* or *most* when comparing three or more nouns.

    A **preposition** is a word that relates a noun or pronoun to another word in a sentence.

    A **prepositional phrase** is a group of words that begins with a preposition and ends with a noun. It can function as an adjective.

- **Introduce the Adjectives and Prepositions Mini-Chart**

    Give each student an Adjectives and Prepositions Mini-Chart (page 47). Review the word lists, and clarify the meaning of any words with which students may be unfamiliar.

Guided Learning

Have students complete the activities on pages 48–49 before assigning the independent practice pages. Check for understanding by circulating around the classroom during guided learning.

Independent Learning

- **What a Good Deal! (page 54):** Point out that only a few number words (e.g., one/single/lone, two/pair, three/triplet) have replacements that do not change the meaning of the sentence.
- **An Exhibit of Interest (page 55):** Refer students to the mini-chart for prepositions that signal a phrase.
- **Easier or Harder? (page 56):** Students should circle *easier, poorest, more perfect, Best, longer, more difficult, cooler, busiest, shorter, most tired, richer, fattest, most expensive, coldest,* and *more successful.*
- **A Book Review (page 57):** Students should write, in order, *best, better, good, bad, less, little, Most, worse, many, worst, More,* and *least.*

Wrap-Up

Have students write a story where the setting is crucial to the plot. Tell them to include many descriptive adjectives and phrases that will help the reader visualize where the story takes place.

Adjectives and Prepositions Mini-Chart

An **adjective** is a word that describes a noun or pronoun. The "worn-out" adjectives in the top row can be replaced with one of the more vivid words shown below.

big	small	good	bad	smart
huge	puny	great	horrendous	brilliant
gigantic	little	fantastic	awful	brainy
immense	tiny	stupendous	horrid	intelligent
large	wee	fine	lousy	bright
colossal	miniature	excellent	disturbing	quick
important	minute	beneficial	inferior	clever

A **comparative adjective** compares two nouns. A **superlative adjective** compares three or more nouns.

Adjective	Comparative	Superlative
flat	flatter	flattest
funny	funnier	funniest
difficult	more difficult	most difficult
exciting	more exciting	most exciting

Some adjectives have **irregular comparative** and **superlative forms.**

Adjective	Comparative	Superlative
good	better	best
bad	worse	worst
much, many	more	most
little	less	least

A **preposition** is a word that relates a noun or pronoun to another word in a sentence.

about	above	across	after	against
around	as	at	before	behind
below	beside	between	beyond	by
down	during	for	from	in
into	of	on	over	through
to	toward	under	until	up
with	within	without	inside	outside

A **prepositional phrase** begins with a preposition and ends with a noun.
An **adjective prepositional phrase** modifies another noun in the sentence.

Pictures <u>of flowers</u> lined the walls.   *of flowers* modifies *pictures*
A photograph <u>of a baby</u> was displayed on the shelf.   *of a baby* modifies *photograph*

Objective

Students will choose more descriptive adjectives to replace overused adjectives.

Materials

- Descriptive Adjectives reproducible (page 50)
- overhead projector/ transparency

Descriptive Adjectives

Copy the Descriptive Adjectives reproducible onto an overhead transparency, and display it. Tell students that adjectives are words that describe a person, a place, a thing, or an idea. Read aloud the sentences one at a time, and ask volunteers to underline the adjectives. Then, have students read the underlined adjectives and state if any of them are commonly overused. Have students circle the commonly overused adjectives *good* and *bad*. Invite volunteers to replace the overused adjectives with more descriptive adjectives and write them above the circled words.

Prepositional Phrases

Objective

Students will determine if the adjective prepositional phrase describes *what kind* or *which one*.

Materials

- Adjectives and Prepositions Mini-Chart (page 47)
- Prepositional Phrases reproducible (page 51)
- colored pencils

Give each student a copy of the Adjectives and Prepositions Mini-Chart. Point out the list of prepositions. Tell students that a preposition relates a noun or pronoun to another word in the sentence. Explain that they can look for these prepositions as they identify prepositional phrases. Tell students that prepositional phrases can act as adjectives. These phrases describe another noun in the sentence. Explain that if a prepositional phrase is removed from the sentence, the sentence will still be complete. Give each student a Prepositional Phrases reproducible. Ask volunteers to read aloud each sentence. Have students underline the prepositional phrases with a red pencil. Ask volunteers to share what the phrase describes and circle the noun it describes with a blue pencil. Invite volunteers to complete the chart by writing the underlined prepositional phrases and the word each phrase describes. *(Students should list 1.* **of the Old West** *describes* **Cowboys** *2.* **who worked the trail drives** *describes* **person** *and* **from Texas** *describes* **trail** *3.* **with long horns** *describes* **cattle** *4.* **with ropes** *describes* **experts** *5.* **on the ground** *describes* **campfire** *6.* **under their seat** *describes* **saddle** *and* **of equipment** *describes* **piece** *7.* **on their feet** *describes* **boots** *8.* **in the stirrup** *describes* **foot** *9.* **of the boot** *describes* **top** *10.* **on the high boot top** *describes* **stitching**.)

Comparing with Adjectives

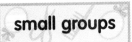
Copy the Comparing with Adjectives reproducible on card stock, and cut apart the word cards. Give each student a word card. Tell students they are to walk around the classroom and try to find classmates who have either the adjective, comparative adjective, or superlative adjective for their word. Students should end up in groups of three. Once all groups are formed, give each group a piece of writing paper. Have each group create three sentences, one for each word. Tell students the sentences must be related and correctly use the adjective form. Have groups share their sentences with the class.

Objective

Students will use the correct form of comparative and superlative adjectives in sentences.

Materials

- Comparing with Adjectives reproducible (page 52)
- card stock
- scissors
- writing paper

Using the Correct Form

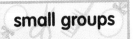
Write the following adjectives in a column on the board: *good, bad, much/many,* and *little.* Explain that these words are adjectives and they describe nouns. However, their comparative and superlative forms are not made by adding *-er/-est* or *more/most.* Their forms are new words. Give each student a copy of the Adjectives and Prepositions Mini-Chart. Point out that the comparative and superlative forms of the adjectives *good, bad, much/many,* and *little* are listed on the chart. Read aloud the poem on the Using the Correct Adjective Form reproducible. Divide the class into small groups. Give each group a copy of the poem. Ask group members to look at each line of the poem to see if they can find the comparative and superlative forms of the adjectives listed on the board in the poem. Have groups circle each comparative adjective and underline each superlative adjective they find. Ask group members to share the words they circled. Record student responses on the board. Point out that these adjectives are often overused, but when the form of these adjectives changes, the words do not get repetitive in a passage.

Objective

Students will identify the correct form of the irregular adjectives *good, bad, much/many,* and *little.*

Materials

- Adjectives and Prepositions Mini-Chart (page 47)
- Using the Correct Adjective Form reproducible (page 53)

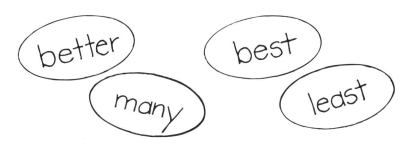

Descriptive Adjectives

1. Vincent Van Gogh was a good painter.

2. His beautiful paintings displayed many emotions.

3. His early pictures were dark and moody.

4. Van Gogh wanted to show the bad poverty of poor people he knew.

5. Van Gogh went to live with his helpful brother in the beautiful city of Paris.

6. New art movements were arising in stylish Paris.

7. The good painter experimented with smart colors and heavy strokes.

8. He painted scenes of sunny fields, big trees, good peasants, and country life.

9. The older Van Gogh was often unhappy.

10. His good paintings were not popular until after his untimely death.

Writing Makeovers • 5–6 © 2003 Creative Teaching Press

Prepositional Phrases

1. Cowboys of the Old West were a rugged bunch.

2. A cowboy was a person who worked the trail drives from Texas.

3. Cowboys were careful of cattle with long horns.

4. They became experts with ropes.

5. A campfire on the ground kept them warm at night.

6. The saddle under their seat was an important piece of equipment.

7. The boots on their feet were a cowboy's pride and joy.

8. The high cut heel kept a foot in the stirrup.

9. The top of the boot was loose so it would come off quickly.

10. The stitching on the high boot top made the leather stand straight up.

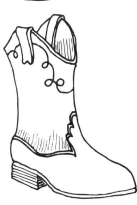

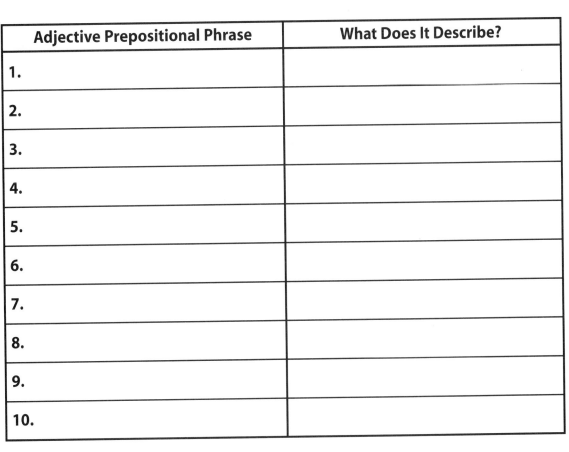

Adjective Prepositional Phrase	What Does It Describe?
1.	
2.	
3.	
4.	
5.	
6.	
7.	
8.	
9.	
10.	

Comparing with Adjectives

tall	taller	tallest
difficult	more difficult	most difficult
colorful	more colorful	most colorful
large	larger	largest
unusual	more unusual	most unusual
numerous	more numerous	most numerous
tiny	tinier	tiniest
long	longer	longest
dark	darker	darkest
swift	swifter	swiftest
graceful	more graceful	most graceful

Writing Makeovers • 5–6 © 2003 Creative Teaching Press

Using the Correct Adjective Form

Directions: Read the poem. Circle the comparative forms and underline the superlative forms of the words **good, bad, much/many,** and **little.** See if you can find all nine.

There once was a child who could be very good,

But often she thought, "I act better than I should."

So bad tricks she would play on those less big than she.

The little ones would cry, "Why are you picking on me?"

And she'd laugh the worst laugh, a deep cackle we hear.

To the wee ones, her motive was worse than they feared.

Then many of the others joined together to plot

And the more that they plotted the louder they got.

They laughed and they played and they had so much fun

And the whole time that horrible child they shunned.

The child then realized she was truly left out.

She wanted to join them and started to shout,

"Please let me join you, I'll be better I swear."

Most others agreed; made her promise right there.

Now they were not afraid of the child in the least.

Seems the wee ones had finally got rid of the beast.

So from then on a GOOD child was part of the rest.

See, the trick of the wee ones by far was the best!

—**Pamela Jennett**

Writing Makeovers • 5–6 © 2003 Creative Teaching Press

Name _____   Date _____

What a Good Deal!

Directions: Read the passage. Underline the adjectives that appear in each sentence. See if you can find all 28. Then, write a more vivid adjective above each "worn-out" adjective.

In 1803, President Jefferson offered to purchase the beautiful city of New Orleans. At that time, New Orleans belonged to powerful France, not the small United States. The surprised Jefferson received word that Napoleon wanted to sell him Louisiana instead! Louisiana was a huge territory. This smart purchase would double the size of the United States.

President Jefferson was excited about this purchase. He immediately sent two young explorers to survey this new land. He chose Meriwether Lewis, a captain in the military. Lewis was honored to lead the unique expedition. Lewis then chose William Clark, a fellow officer, to accompany him. The exploration party consisted of Lewis, Clark, a large group of fellow explorers, a Native American interpreter, a black slave, and Lewis's dog.

The trip was a big success. They explored majestic mountains and wild rivers. They met friendly Native American tribes. They examined and catalogued new species of native plants and wild animals. They made it all the way to the rugged Pacific Ocean. Jefferson thought he had made a smart purchase.

Writing Makeovers • 5–6 © 2003 Creative Teaching Press

An Exhibit of Interest

Directions: Read the passage. Underline the twelve prepositional phrases. Draw an arrow to the noun each prepositional phrase describes.

The bones of the dinosaurs are an interesting exhibit at the museum. Some of the bones are quite large. The bones of the Brachiosaurus weighed 70 tons and stood 39 feet high. Dinosaurs with very small skeletons were also found. The skeleton of the Compsognathus was the weight of a cat. The exhibit near the front door shows how small a dinosaur fossil can be.

Dinosaurs in their natural habitat are exhibited there. Trees and ferns in the background show the appearance of the Earth. The details of the displays are interesting to see.

Easier or Harder?

Directions: Read each sentence. Circle the correct form of the adjective given in parentheses.

1. "Washing cars is (easier, easiest) than babysitting," exclaimed Lisa.

2. Robert replied, "I am the (poorest, most poor) person here."

3. "I'm ready to make some money," echoed Zia. "I can't think of a (perfecter, more perfect) way."

4. The kids made a sign that read, "The (Best, Most Good) Car Wash Here!"

5. In an hour, the line was (longest, longer) than they expected.

6. "This job is (more difficult, difficulter) than I thought," cried Jack.

7. Lisa answered, "At least it is (cooler, coolest) than mowing a lawn!"

8. They were the (most busy, busiest) car wash in town.

9. By afternoon, the line was (more short, shorter) than it had been in the morning.

10. "This is the (most tired, more tired) I have ever been," sighed Avery.

11. "But we are (richest, richer) than we were this morning!" announced Robert.

12. In the cash box, there was the (fatter, fattest) bundle of dollar bills.

13. "I'm going to buy the (expensivest, most expensive) gift!" declared Lisa.

14. "Right now, I just want to buy the (coldest, most cold) drink possible," said Jack.

15. The friends were very tired, but they had never felt (successfuller, more successful).

Writing Makeovers • 5–6 © 2003 Creative Teaching Press

A Book Review

Directions: Read the book review. This passage is missing adjectives. Use context clues in each sentence to figure out what the missing adjective is. Choose a **different** word from the word bank to complete each sentence. Reread the review to check that your new adjectives make sense in context.

Word Bank

good	better	best
bad	worse	worst
many	more	most
little	less	least

I highly recommend *Sand Dunes of Time* by Walter Richey. This is the

_____ book I have ever read. The book is a sequel to

Richey's first book, *A Walk on the Edge*. In my opinion, *Sand Dunes of Time* is the

_____ book of the two. Mr. Richey uses colorful descriptions

that really make the characters come alive. Most authors do not do a very

_____ job developing the setting of the story, but Mr. Richey

paints such a vivid scene, it feels like you are there.

The story begins by introducing the main character, Alonso. The reader meets

Alonso when he is obviously having a _____ day. After a little

while, the reader meets Hanimol, who is _____ a friend than he

is a troublemaker. It takes very _____ time for these two to get

into all kinds of trouble. _____ of the time, these circumstances

would be frustrating, but it is hard not to laugh at Alonso's antics. Just when things

could not get any _____ than they already are, they do.

However, Alonso has as _____ ideas as there are grains of sand

on the beach, and he always finds a solution. When Alonso and Hanimol are faced

with the _____ circumstances you can imagine, they manage to

escape with humor and grace. _____ often than not, you will

find yourself rooting for Alonso to succeed. At the very _____,

the characters that you meet are worth every penny you spend on this book.

Adverbs

This section focuses on adverbs and prepositional phrases that act as adverbs. Adverbs add more detail to writing; in this case, they add detail to the action of the sentence. Adverbs like *very, really,* and *good* are overused. This section helps students find replacements for these overused adverbs.

Getting Started

• Define

An **adverb** is a word that adds details to a verb. An adverb tells *how, how often, when,* or *where* something was done. It can also modify an adjective or another adverb.

A **comparative adverb** compares two actions. A **superlative adverb** compares three or more actions.

An **adverb phrase** is a prepositional phrase that tells more about a verb, another adjective, or another adverb. It tells *how, how often, when,* or *where.*

• Introduce the Adverbs Mini-Chart

Give each student an Adverbs Mini-Chart (page 59). Review the word lists, and clarify the meaning of any words with which students may be unfamiliar.

Guided Learning

Have students complete the activities on pages 60–61 before assigning the independent practice pages. Check for understanding by circulating around the classroom during guided learning.

Independent Learning

- **Overused Adverbs (page 66):** The context of the sentence will help students choose the best word to replace *very* or *really.*
- **Baking Cookies (page 67):** Point out that all of the sentences are imperative.
- **Postcard from Hawaii (page 68):** To extend the activity, have students replace *good* and *well* with more descriptive choices.
- **Your Own Secret Garden (page 69):** Students should list, in order, *harder, most brilliantly, taller, larger, widest, Most carefully, more easily, best, more closely,* and *more rapidly.*

Wrap-Up

Ask students to choose a favorite recipe and bring it to class. (Provide a cookbook for students to select a recipe from, if needed.) Have students rewrite their recipe in paragraph form, giving specific directions on how and when to work with certain ingredients and where actions in the recipe should occur. Tell students to circle the adverbs they included in their writing.

Adverbs Mini-Chart

An **adverb** is a word that adds details to a verb. An adverb tells *how, how often, when,* or *where* something was done. It can also modify an adjective or another adverb.

Many adjectives become adverbs with the addition of the suffix *-ly.*

How	How Often	When	Where
quickly	always	never	near
sluggishly	frequently	usually	outside
sloppily	never	early	here
carefully	often	finally	up
politely	seldom	first	forward

A **comparative adverb** compares two actions. A **superlative adverb** compares three or more actions.

Adverb	Comparative	Superlative
long	longer	longest
early	earlier	earliest
skillfully	more skillfully	most skillfully
slowly	more slowly	most slowly

Some adverbs have **irregular comparative** and **superlative** forms.

Adverb	Comparative	Superlative
well	better	best
badly	worse	worst
much, many	more	most
little	less	least

A **prepositional phrase** begins with a preposition and ends with a noun. An **adverb prepositional phrase** modifies a verb, an adjective, or another adverb in the sentence. Note: Refer to your Adjectives and Prepositions Mini-Chart for a list of prepositions.

An adverb phrase that modifies a verb

We sailed <u>over the glassy lake</u>.   *over the glassy lake* tells **where** they *sailed*

The boy ran <u>without a care</u>.   *without a care* tells **how** the boy *ran*

She read her book <u>in the afternoon</u>.   *in the afternoon* tells **when** she *read*

An adverb phrase that modifies an adjective

He is famous <u>for his invention</u>.   *for his invention* modifies *famous* (an adjective)

An adverb phrase that modifies another adverb

The family drove far <u>into the countryside</u>.   *into the countryside* modifies *far*

Objectives

Students will

- identify adverbs in a sentence
- find synonyms for a list of adverbs

Materials

- ꙮ Recognizing Adverbs reproducible (page 62)
- ꙮ overhead projector/ transparency

Recognizing Adverbs

Copy the Recognizing Adverbs reproducible onto an overhead transparency, and display it. Explain to students that an adverb can modify a verb, an adjective, or another adverb. An adverb tells *how, how often, when,* or *where.* Have a volunteer read aloud the first sentence on the transparency. Ask students what action is occurring in the predicate. *(studied)* Then, ask students if there is a word that tells *how, how often, when,* or *where. (hard)* Explain that *hard* is the adverb and that it modifies *studied.* Underline *hard,* and add it to the chart at the bottom of the transparency. Have students think of another adverb that means *hard* (e.g., *intensely*). Add the new word to the chart next to *hard.* Repeat with the remaining sentences. *(Students should locate and underline 1. hard 2. extremely 3. swiftly 4. long 5. earlier 6. recently 7. quickly 8. briefly 9. loudly 10. politely 11. well and really 12. skillfully 13. very 14. next 15. slightly.)*

Objective

Students will identify adverb prepositional phrases and use them correctly in sentences.

Materials

- ꙮ Prepositional Phrases as Adverbs reproducible (page 63)
- ꙮ card stock
- ꙮ scissors

Prepositional Phrases as Adverbs

Copy the Prepositional Phrases as Adverbs reproducible on card stock, and cut apart the phrase cards. Give each student a card. Review some words that act as prepositions, such as *into, through, on, in, of,* and *with.* Tell students to create a sentence that correctly uses the prepositional phrase from their card. Have students share their sentence with the class. Ask volunteers to identify the adverb phrase and say if it tells *how, how often, when,* or *where.* If time permits, invite students to exchange cards and create a sentence with a new prepositional phrase.

by workers	**on the bus**

Good or Well?

pairs

Copy the Good or Well? reproducible onto an overhead transparency. Copy a class set of the reproducible. Tell students that *good* is often misused as an adverb. Explain that *good* is an adjective that modifies nouns and *well* is an adverb that tells how something was done. Display the transparency. Read the sentences for number one together as a class. Invite volunteers to complete the two sentences. Divide the class into pairs. Give each student a reproducible. Have partners read each sentence and circle the word that is being modified. Then, have them select the correct adjective or adverb and write it on the line. (*Students should write* 1. **good, well** 2. **well, good** 3. **well, good** 4. **good, well** 5. **well, good** 6. **well, good** 7. **good, well** 8. **good, well** 9. **good, well** 10. **good, well.**)

Objective

Students will recognize the difference between the adjective *good* and the adverb *well*.

Materials

- Good or Well? reproducible (page 64)
- overhead projector/ transparency

Comparing with Adverbs

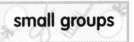
small groups

Copy the Comparing with Adverbs reproducible onto an overhead transparency, and make a copy for each small group of students. Display the transparency. Tell students that the advertisement uses lots of comparative adverbs to describe the product. Read the advertisement together. Divide the class into small groups. Give each group a reproducible. Ask group members to look for and circle the comparative and superlative adverbs on their reproducible. Remind students that comparative adverbs are made by adding *-er* or *more* and superlative adverbs are made by adding *-est* or *most*. Have students look for these clues when trying to find adverbs that tell *how, how often, when,* or *where*. Have students record the three forms of each circled word at the bottom of the reproducible. For example, *soon, sooner, soonest.* (*Students should locate and circle* **sooner, better, most eagerly, more heavily, better, longer, more often, most completely,** *and* **more tasty.**)

Objective

Students will identify comparative or superlative forms of an adverb.

Materials

- Comparing with Adverbs reproducible (page 65)
- overhead projector/ transparency

Recognizing Adverbs

1. Amanda and Sherry studied hard for their speech on Friday.

2. That afternoon, the library was extremely quiet.

3. Sherry ran swiftly home in the pouring rain.

4. She worked long into the night.

5. The next morning, she woke earlier than usual.

6. Sherry recently bought a new skirt and decided to wear it.

7. She dressed quickly and ate her breakfast.

8. Sherry stopped briefly at the corner to wait for Amanda.

9. The school bell rang loudly, startling the girls.

10. Amanda nodded politely as she was called to the podium.

11. Amanda spoke well and the audience appeared really interested.

12. Her charts had been skillfully drawn.

13. Sherry thought Amanda's speech was very good.

14. It was Sherry's turn to speak next.

15. Sherry did not feel even slightly nervous.

1.		9.	
2.		10.	
3.		11.	
4.		12.	
5.		13.	
6.		14.	
7.		15.	
8.			

Prepositional Phrases as Adverbs

by remote control	toward the finish line	for many years
in the bicycle lane	until dawn	on the bus
above the roof	around the racetrack	with remarkable speed
between two rocks	through the night	as the sun came up
with style	as quickly as possible	during the windstorm
with curiosity	toward the end of the day	around the lake
for an hour	by workers	into the boxes

Name _____   Date _____

Good or Well?

Directions: Read each sentence and circle the word that is being modified. Write **good** or **well** on each blank line.

1. Stacy read a _____ book.

   She reads very _____.

2. The boys' track team placed _____ at the track meet.

   They ran a _____ race.

3. The child was tired, but he still behaved _____.

   Because of his _____ behavior, he received an ice-cream cone.

4. Grandmother and Aunt Arlene had a _____trip.

   They travel _____ together.

5. I was not feeling _____.

   I did not have a _____ day.

6. Mark and his brother Matthew work _____ together.

   Their _____ work will be rewarded.

7. My puppy knows a _____trick.

   He participates _____ in his obedience class.

8. Mr. Martinez is a _____ salesperson.

   He sells _____ under pressure.

9. This meal was very _____.

   My mom cooks _____.

10. We came up with a _____ plan for our project.

    We planned _____ and now it shows in our final work.

Writing Makeovers • 5–6 © 2003 Creative Teaching Press

Names _____   Date _____

Comparing with Adverbs

Directions: Circle the comparative and superlative adverbs. You should find nine. Write the three forms of each circled word on the lines below.

The sooner you buy them, the better your breakfast!

Dandy Candy Flakes

Children most eagerly sit down to breakfast if they know they will be having Dandy Candy Flakes. Each spoonful is more heavily loaded with flavor than ever before. Dandy Candy Flakes taste better than 90% of other children's breakfast cereals. They stay crunchy longer in milk. Children will want breakfast more often.

Mom! This is the most completely fortified cereal on the market!

Now More Tasty Flavor in Every Box!

_____

_____

_____

_____

_____

_____

_____

Overused Adverbs

Directions: The adverbs **very** and **really** are overused in writing. Read the article and underline **very** and **really** each time you read them. Select words from the word bank to replace these overused words. Write a new word above each underlined word. Use each new word only once. Reread the article to make sure your new adverbs makes sense in context.

Word Bank

awfully	exceptionally	extraordinarily	extremely	definitely
fantastically	incredibly	marvelously	quite	obviously
undeniably	unusually	wonderfully	exceedingly	
especially	greatly	immensely	actually	

Local Bicyclist Wins Race

GILCREST   Scott Upton, a really talented cyclist, posted his first win in a 50-mile (31-kilometer) race yesterday. He very easily pulled ahead of the other cyclists to take first place in the last 5 miles (8.1 kilometers). Scott says, "I train really hard, and I get very good results. I really expected to do this well." Mr. Upton may have expected to win, but the crowd was very surprised. Most of the audience remembered the really horrible crash Upton suffered a year ago. "I was very surprised to see Scott here," remarked Officer Lewis. " I really thought he'd be very slow." Really, Scott surprised everyone. What are his plans for next year? "I'll keep training very hard, and I'll be back," Upton replied. "You just see if I don't do very well next year!"

Writing Makeovers • 5–6 © 2003 Creative Teaching Press

Baking Cookies

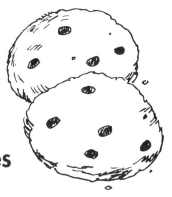

Directions: Read the cookie recipe. Underline the 14 adverb prepositional phrases. Write each phrase in the correct column in the chart below.

Chocolate Chip Oatmeal Cookies

1 cup butter   1 teaspoon vanilla   1 teaspoon salt

1½ cups sugar   1½ cups flour   1 cup chocolate chips

2 eggs   1 teaspoon baking soda   2 cups oatmeal

Before you begin, preheat the oven to 375°F. Collect the ingredients and place them on the counter. Soften the butter in the microwave oven. Then place the butter and sugar into a large bowl. Mix these ingredients together until no lumps remain. Stir in eggs and vanilla.

Sift flour, baking soda, and salt together onto a paper plate. Pour the sifted ingredients over the butter mixture. Stir well until you have a stiff batter. Now add the chocolate chips and oatmeal to the batter. Roll into balls and set on the cookie sheet. Bake for 10 minutes. Let the cookies cool and then enjoy them with a large glass of milk.

When?	Where?	How?

Postcard from Hawaii

Directions: Read the message on the postcard. Underline at least ten adverbs. Also, the words **good** and **well** are sometimes mixed up and used incorrectly. Fix the incorrect words by using **good** or **well** correctly in the sentences.

Dear Robyn,

We are having such a well time! It was a very long plane ride. The plane flew smoothly so I wasn't too afraid. On Tuesday, I excitedly took a Hula lesson. The instructor said I danced quite good. We went to a luau last night for dinner. We ate slowly when the show began. All of the dancers moved very good. The lights flashed brightly and the beat of the music remained solidly in my memory. We had a well evening. I hope you are behaving good without me! See you soon.

Your friend,

Laurie

Your Own Secret Garden

Directions: Read the paragraph. Use the correct comparative or superlative form of an adverb from the word bank to complete each sentence. Reread the story to make sure your choices make sense in context.

Word Bank

more brilliantly	more carefully	more closely	taller	larger
most brilliantly	most carefully	most closely	tallest	largest
wider	better	harder	more easily	more rapidly
widest	best	hardest	most easily	most rapidly

Building your own secret garden is no _____ than digging a hole. First,
find a location were the sun shines _____ during the whole day.
Find four long poles. The poles need to stand _____ than you do. Draw a
square on the ground. Trace it _____ than the space you take up when you are
sitting cross-legged. Join the four poles together at the top end with twine. Place each
of the other ends at one of the four corners of your square. It will look like a tepee. The
front, where you enter, should measure the _____. _____,
wind string between the poles so they are enclosed. Leave the front open so you can
sit inside _____ than you can if it were closed. On the ground between
the poles, drag a trowel to draw the _____ straight trench you can. In the
trench, plant bean seeds. No bean seed should be _____ planted than
the width of your hand. Cover the seeds with dirt and water well. Bean vines grow
_____ than other vines. They will quickly cover the twine and poles to create
your own secret hideaway.

Spelling

This section focuses on how spelling affects the meaning of a passage. Students will learn that poor spelling interferes with the reader's ability to understand the writer's message. In addition, students will learn strategies for remembering the correct spelling of frequently misspelled words. Students will discriminate between correctly and incorrectly spelled words in context.

Getting Started

- **Introduce the Spelling Mini-Chart**

    Give each student a Spelling Mini-Chart (page 71). Review the word lists, and clarify the meaning of any words with which students may be unfamiliar.

Guided Learning

Have students complete the activities on pages 72–73 before assigning the independent practice pages. Check for understanding by circulating around the classroom during guided learning.

Independent Learning

- **Musical Vibrations (page 76):** Encourage students to use the mini-chart to check word spellings. Also, point out that the correct spelling of a word may appear elsewhere on the page.
- **The Fox and the Hen (page 77):** Point out that the correct spelling of a word may appear elsewhere in the passage. Students should find the misspelled words *whent, culd, wus, thout, wright, meel, haft, abot, Hellow, callt, arround, vary, wheather, becuse,* and *frends.*
- **Make the Right Choice (page 78):** Students should shade in 1. *D* 2. *B* 3. *A* 4. *D* 5. *A* 6. *B* 7. *C* 8. *D* 9. *B* 10. *D.*
- **The Fresco Painters (page 79):** Students should list *beautiful* or *special, pictures, beautiful* or *special, ceilings, Because, first, loose, carefully, already, piece, through, connects, Finally, complete, before,* and *enough.*
- **Letter to a Friend (page 80):** Remind students that only the homophones are misspelled.

Wrap-Up

Have students write a personal narrative about a science project which they have participated in or would like to participate in. Tell students to include details about the project. Ask them to include the correct vocabulary related to the science project. Encourage them to use a dictionary for any words they are not sure they know how to spell.

Spelling Mini-Chart

Frequently Misspelled Words

address	country	friend	little	quarter	tomorrow
✓ again	cousin	goes	✓ loose	quiet	trouble
all right	decorate	government	✓ lose	quit	truly
✓ already	definite	great	maintenance	quite	Tuesday
although	desert	guarantee	many	raise	until
✓ always	dessert	guard	mathematics	really	use
angry	dictionary	guess	money	receive	usually
animal	doctor	half	myself	recess	vacation
another	does	handkerchief	necessary	remember	valentine
answer	early	handsome	neighbor	rhyme	very
aunt	embarrass	height	neither	rhythm	was
bargain	enough	hello	nickel	rough	Wednesday
beautiful	environment	hospital	niece	said	weigh
because	everybody	hour	occasion	school	weird
been	everyone	house	occurrence	science	went
believe	everything	independence	of	scissors	were
bought	exaggerate	instead	off	secretary	what
built	excited	into	often	separate	when
business	familiar	judgment	once	sign	white
calendar	family	kindergarten	only	since	who
caught	father	know	people	sincerely	with
character	favorite	knowledge	picture	straight	women
chief	February	laboratory	piece	success	work
children	fierce	later	please	sugar	would
chocolate	finally	laugh	potatoes	surprise	
clothes	first	library	practice	teacher	
conscious	foreign	license	pretty	terrible	
cough	forty	lightning	privilege	though	
could	fourth	listen	probably	through	

explain

Homophones are words that sound alike but have different spellings and meanings.

to	right	their	wood	eight	which
too	write	there	would	ate	witch
two		they're			

whole	your	who's	where	piece	knew
hole	you're	whose	wear	peace	new

Sound It Like It Spells

whole class

Objective

Students will use various strategies to help them remember how to spell difficult words.

Materials

- Spelling Mini-Chart (page 71)
- index cards

Write the word *beautiful* on the board. Tell students that some words are spelled differently than we pronounce them. However, explain that if students use sound clues to help them spell, they will remember the spelling of the word better. Write *be-a-yoo-ti-ful* underneath the word *beautiful*. Tell students that this is a clue for spelling *beautiful*. Explain to students that if they sound out each letter that is not heard, they will remember all of the letters. Give each student a copy of the Spelling Mini-Chart and two index cards. Assign or have students choose two words with silent letters from the mini-chart. Have students write each word on an index card. Have them break apart each word into sounds to help them remember the letters and write the sounds on the back of the cards. For example, *science* becomes *sky-ens-ee, friend* becomes *fry-end,* or *enough* becomes *ee-no-ugh.* Invite students to trade cards and practice spelling the words on their new cards. As time permits, have students continue trading cards.

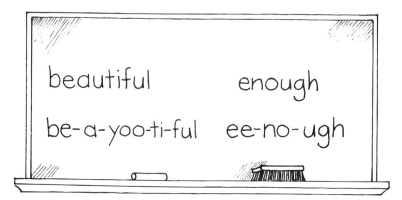

Words That Sound Silly

whole class

Objective

Students will discuss how misspelled words change or obscure the intended meaning of a sentence.

Materials

- Words That Sound Silly reproducible (page 74)
- overhead projector/ transparency

Copy the Words That Sound Silly reproducible onto an overhead transparency, and display it. Read aloud the first sentence. Ask the class if they think there is anything wrong with this sentence. Select volunteers to share their thoughts. Point out that based on the way this sentence is written, *Grandmother* is asking the reader to be the animal *deer.* Explain that *deer* is a homophone for another word. Have a volunteer spell the correct homophone for the sentence. Draw a line through *deer,* and replace it with *dear.* Continue to read each sentence and have volunteers explain the meaning of the given homophone and what it should really say. Record the correct homophone above each sentence. *(Students should locate **deer, right, knot, threw, overdo, our, bare, roll, male, plane, knew, piece, blew, so, peace, whole,** and **genes.**)*

Oh, Those Silent Letters

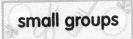
Give each student an Oh, Those Silent Letters reproducible. Explain that many English words have tricky spellings that involve silent letters. Read aloud the words for problem number one. Ask students to identify the letter cluster and silent letter that the three words have in common. Invite a volunteer to read aloud the statement below the first three words. The student should say *These words have the letter cluster sch and the h is silent.* Divide the class into small groups. Have students complete the rest of the reproducible. Then, have students use dictionaries to look up and verify other words that have the same letter clusters where the same letter is silent. Remind them to check the pronunciation key to verify the silent letter.

Objective
Students will identify word groups that have the same difficult spellings.

Materials
- Oh, Those Silent Letters reproducible (page 75)
- dictionaries

Hear a Homophone, See a Homophone

Write the homophones from the Spelling Mini-Chart on separate index cards. Distribute one card to each student. Say *If you have the word would, please stand and hold it up.* Two students should stand. One student will have *wood* and the other student *would.* Point out that these words are homophones. Explain that these words have the same sounds but the meaning is different. Have the students correctly use their word in a sentence. Once all matches are made, give each pair of students a piece of construction paper. Have partners create a poster that illustrates the meaning of their homophones and includes the words. Invite pairs to share their poster with the class.

Objective
Students will use visual clues to help them remember the meanings of homophones.

Materials
- Spelling Mini-Chart (page 71)
- index cards
- construction paper
- crayons or markers

Words That Sound Silly

1. Grandmother said, "Please be a deer and make me a cup of tea."

2. Terry remarked, "I learned to right in kindergarten."

3. "I have knot been feeling very well," whined my little sister.

4. "Put this rope threw your dog's collar," instructed the trainer.

5. "Uh oh, my book is overdo at the library," commented Tony.

6. "It took me an our to mow the lawn," I replied.

7. On our vacation, we saw a bare on the side of the road.

8. Jeanette announced, "I'm getting a good roll in the school play!"

9. Jenny sent her money by male.

10. "I don't like how plane my hairstyle is," moaned Rita.

11. Our family got a knew car last night," bragged Kelly.

12. The Jacksons enjoyed the piece and quiet at the lake.

13. "That blew dress looks like something I want," declared Amie.

14. She will so a peace of fabric over the whole in her genes.

Writing Makeovers • 5–6 © 2003 Creative Teaching Press

Name _____   Date _____

Oh, Those Silent Letters

Directions: Read each set of words. Find the letter cluster and silent letter for each set of words.

1. schedule   school   schooner

   These words have the letter cluster _____ and the _____ is silent.

2. character   echo   chaos

   These words have the letter cluster _____ and the _____ is silent.

3. guess   guild   guitar

   These words have the letter cluster _____ and the _____ is silent.

4. know   knit   jackknife

   These words have the letter cluster _____ and the _____ is silent.

5. nightly   laughter   haughty

   These words have the letter cluster _____ and the _____ is silent.

6. folklore   yolk   walking

   These words have the letter cluster _____ and the _____ is silent.

7. sign   reign   gnaw

   These words have the letter cluster _____ and the _____ is silent.

Musical Vibrations

Directions: Each sentence contains one spelling error. Read each sentence and underline the misspelled word. Rewrite the word correctly on the line.

1. Can you make music with your favorit drinking glass?   _____

2. Find a glass with exceptionly smooth sides and a smooth rim.   _____

3. Alwase make sure your fingers are free of grease.   _____

4. Be sure and wash your hands relly well.   _____

5. Place a small amont of water in the bottom of the glass.   _____

6. Yuse water to moisten the end of your finger.   _____

7. With grate care, place the tip of your finger on the rim of the glass.   _____

8. Rub your finger in a circular moshun.   _____

9. Did you here a tone right away?   _____

10. You mite have to rub a little longer.   _____

11. If it dosen't work, try changing your speed.   _____

12. You can allways change the pressure, too.   _____

13. If you still hear no sound, try a diffrent glass.   _____

14. If the glass is too thick, it wun't work.   _____

15. Anybody can make this beatiful musical instrument.   _____

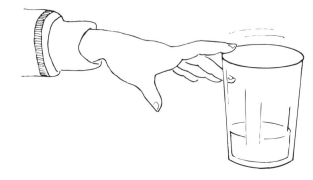

Writing Makeovers • 5–6 © 2003 Creative Teaching Press

The Fox and the Hen

Directions: Read the fable. Circle the 15 misspelled words. Write each word correctly in the chart below.

Late one night, Fox whent out to look for some dinner. He came upon a henhouse, and he knew that there must be hens inside. Through the open door, up on the highest perch, he culd indeed see a hen. But she wus far out of reach.

Fox thout to himself, "I have to play this wright or there will be no meel for me. She will haft to come to me as I could never reach her." So he thought abot what to do. Before long he had come up with a plan.

"Hellow there, my dear friend Hen," he callt out anxiously. "I haven't seen you arround much lately. Someone told me that you are sick. I am vary worried about you. If you could step down here, I will take your temperature. Then I will know what to do to help you get better."

"Oh, it is so true, my dear Fox," replied Hen. "I have indeed been under the wheather. I appreciate your concern. However, I am better off resting here becuse if I come down for your treatment, it will surely be the death of me."

The moral of the story is: Beware of frends that are not sincere.

Misspelled words spelled correctly:

Make the Right Choice

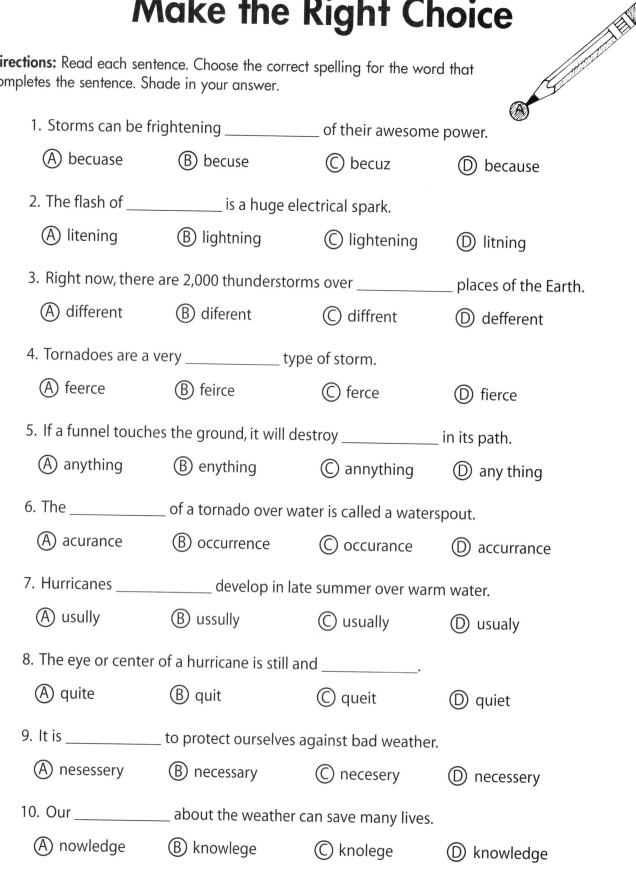

Directions: Read each sentence. Choose the correct spelling for the word that completes the sentence. Shade in your answer.

1. Storms can be frightening _____ of their awesome power.

   Ⓐ becuase   Ⓑ becuse   Ⓒ becuz   Ⓓ because

2. The flash of _____ is a huge electrical spark.

   Ⓐ litening   Ⓑ lightning   Ⓒ lightening   Ⓓ litning

3. Right now, there are 2,000 thunderstorms over _____ places of the Earth.

   Ⓐ different   Ⓑ diferent   Ⓒ diffrent   Ⓓ defferent

4. Tornadoes are a very _____ type of storm.

   Ⓐ feerce   Ⓑ feirce   Ⓒ ferce   Ⓓ fierce

5. If a funnel touches the ground, it will destroy _____ in its path.

   Ⓐ anything   Ⓑ enything   Ⓒ annything   Ⓓ any thing

6. The _____ of a tornado over water is called a waterspout.

   Ⓐ acurance   Ⓑ occurrence   Ⓒ occurance   Ⓓ accurrance

7. Hurricanes _____ develop in late summer over warm water.

   Ⓐ usully   Ⓑ ussully   Ⓒ usually   Ⓓ usualy

8. The eye or center of a hurricane is still and _____.

   Ⓐ quite   Ⓑ quit   Ⓒ queit   Ⓓ quiet

9. It is _____ to protect ourselves against bad weather.

   Ⓐ nesessery   Ⓑ necessary   Ⓒ necesery   Ⓓ necessery

10. Our _____ about the weather can save many lives.

   Ⓐ nowledge   Ⓑ knowlege   Ⓒ knolege   Ⓓ knowledge

Writing Makeovers • 5–6 © 2003 Creative Teaching Press

The Fresco Painters

Directions: Draw an X over the eight misspelled words in the word bank. Rewrite them correctly in the blank boxes. Read the story. Use each word from the word bank only once to complete the sentences in the story. Reread the story to make sure your choice makes sense in context.

Word Bank

byootiful	carfully	through	
beecus	allready	finilly	
ceilings	special	enuff	
first	loose	before	
pichtures	connects		
pieze	complete		

Have you ever had the chance to see the _____ paintings on the ceilings of churches or cathedrals? Have you ever seen the _____ painted by Michelangelo? These _____ paintings are called frescoes. Frescoes are painted on the walls and _____ of buildings. _____ they are so large, frescoes require a special technique.

At _____, a worker chips the plaster on the surface to be painted. He roughens it up with a hammer and removes any _____ pieces. Then, remaining plaster is moistened with water. A new layer of plaster is applied. This layer is _____ smoothed so the surface is completely flat.

The artist has _____ drawn the figure or scene he wants to paint on a large _____ of paper. He outlines the shapes with pinpricks. The paper is then held up to the surface and charcoal dust is blown _____ the pinpricks. An out-line of the image is transferred onto the wall. The artist _____ the dots with a brush dipped in ink. _____, the outline is filled in with colored plaster until the painting is _____.

The painting must be finished _____ the plaster dries. Therefore, only _____ fresh plaster is applied on the wall for one day's painting.

Letter to a Friend

Directions: Underline the 15 misspelled homophones in the letter below. Write the correct homophone above each underlined word.

Dear Jessica,

I thought I would right you a letter. My class just returned home from science camp. This year it was at a knew site and our cabins were grate! Even though it was a lot of fun, I also learned a lot. The first knight we sat outside under the stars and listened two the sounds. I could here the call of a barn owl. The second day we hiked up to Cascade Point. The view was beautiful. We could sea the mountains in the distance as well as the entire valley. A red-tailed hawk flu by. We identified it by the red feathers on its tale. An our later we were back at camp. All of that hiking made me so hungry. I ate to turkey sandwiches. That afternoon we hiked threw the forest. Our leader showed us a Jeffrey pine tree. If you peel a peace of bark, it smells like vanilla. Then we sat inside a medicine wheel. I now no that a medicine wheel was a ceremonial circle used by Native Americans. The morning of the third day we cleaned hour cabins and took pictures. I learned so much. Write back!

Your friend,

Anna

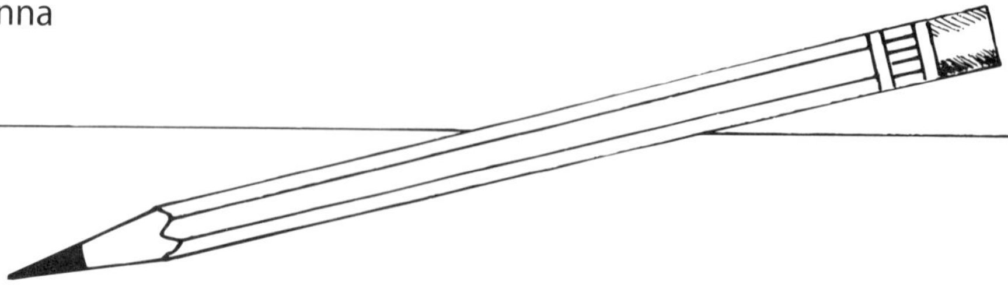

Writing Makeovers • 5–6 © 2003 Creative Teaching Press

Capitalization and Punctuation

This section focuses on how punctuation affects the meaning of a passage. Students will see how punctuation can add emotion and interest to writing. They will also see how a lack of punctuation interferes with the reader's ability to understand and visualize the writer's message. Students will identify and provide missing punctuation. Students will proofread passages for errors in punctuation and capitalization.

Getting Started
- **Introduce the Capitalization and Punctuation Mini-Chart**

    Give each student a Capitalization and Punctuation Mini-Chart (page 82). Review the rules, and clarify any with which students may be unfamiliar. Refer back to the Sentences Mini-Chart (page 7) to review examples of the different types of sentences.

Guided Learning

Have students complete the activities on pages 83—86 before assigning the independent practice pages. Check for understanding by circulating around the classroom during guided learning.

Independent Learning
- **Using Apostrophes (page 89):** Review with the class the rules for using an apostrophe. Also, discuss the use of contractions in writing. Students should list the contractions *let's, you're, we'd, she'll, they've, it's, who's,* and *I'm.*
- **Using Colons (page 90):** Review with the class the rules for using colons correctly.

Wrap-Up

Have each student write a dialogue between himself or herself and a friend about a trip that they would like to take together. Tell students to correctly use quotation marks in their writing and to check for proper capitalization and punctuation. Also, remind them to replace worn-out dialogue words, such as *said* and *asked,* with more "exciting" words.

Capitalization and Punctuation Mini-Chart

A sentence must begin with a capital letter and end with an end mark.

Rules for Capital Letters

Capitalize
- the first word of a sentence
- days of the week and months
- names of holidays
- the pronoun "I"
- proper nouns that name a specific person, place, or thing
- first, last, and important words in titles of books and movies
- abbreviations for states
- greeting and closing of a letter
- first word of a direct quotation

Rules for Punctuation

Use commas
- between a city and state
- in a date
- after the greeting and closing in a letter
- in a series
- with direct quotations
- with appositives and interjections

San Francisco, California
September 23, 1960
Dear Jose,   Your friend,
I buy cherries, oranges, and apples.
"I'm hot," said Jim.
Bryce Canyon, a park, is beautiful.
Hey, you have my book.

Use quotation marks
- around a direct quotation

She called, "Watch out!"

Use apostrophes
- in a contraction
- with possessive nouns

can't   won't   you'll   they've
Susan's coat   the horse's saddle

Use colons
- after the greeting in a business letter
- before a series of items

Dear Sir or Madam:
You will need these items: pen, paper, and glue.

Writing Makeovers • 5–6 © 2003 Creative Teaching Press

Using Capitalization

Copy the Capitalization and Punctuation Mini-Chart and the Using Capitalization reproducible onto overhead transparencies. Ask students to brainstorm capitalization rules. List student responses on the board. Display the mini-chart transparency. Invite students to compare the rules listed on the board with the rules on the mini-chart. Ask for volunteers to point out any rules students did not already think of. Display the Using Capitalization transparency. Ask a volunteer to read aloud the first sentence. Tell students that one of the capitalization rules was not followed in this sentence. Have a volunteer point out the mistake and rewrite the word or words correctly above the incorrect word. Ask a volunteer to explain the capitalization rule needed to make the sentence correct. Write the rule on the line next to the sentence. Continue the activity with the rest of the sentences.

Objective

Students will identify and apply the rules of capitalization to make corrections in sentences.

Materials

- ✎ Capitalization and Punctuation Mini-Chart (page 82)
- ✎ Using Capitalization reproducible (page 87)
- ✎ overhead projector/ transparencies

Using Commas

whole class

Copy the Using Commas reproducible onto an overhead transparency, and display it. Have volunteers read aloud each rule for comma usage. Read the example next to the first rule. Explain to the class that the sentence is missing its commas. Invite a volunteer to add commas to the sentence. Repeat with the remaining sentences.

Objectives

Students will
- identify the rules of using commas
- apply the comma punctuation rules to sentences

Materials

- ✎ Using Commas reproducible (page 88)
- ✎ overhead projector/ transparency

Quotation Marks and Dialogue

Objective

Students will identify, properly punctuate, and capitalize direct quotations.

Materials

- script from a play
- scissors
- sentence strips

In advance, find a script from a play in a language arts or drama book, and make a copy of it. Cut the play into strips, and separate each character's lines. Give each student a strip. Tell students that each strip contains words spoken by a character in a play. Explain that they will turn the sentences into a direct quote. Remind students that a direct quote contains the exact words someone says and is set inside quotation marks. The first word of a quote is capitalized and the end of the quote needs end punctuation. Write a sentence from the play on the board, and add quotation marks. Point out that in some cases a comma is used as end punctuation. For example, *"The river is too high to cross,"* *cried the frog.* Give each student a sentence strip. Have students rewrite their line on the sentence strip and change it into a direct quotation. Collect the completed sentence strips, and display them for the class. Discuss with students the types of punctuation used to complete each sentence.

> "The river is too high to cross," cried the frog.

Apostrophes and Colons

Objective

Students will correctly identify the use of apostrophes and colons.

Materials

- Capitalization and Punctuation Mini-Chart (page 82)
- overhead projector/ transparency

Copy the Capitalization and Punctuation Mini-Chart onto an overhead transparency, and display it. Read and discuss with the class the rules for using apostrophes and colons. Ask volunteers to share an example of each rule. Record student responses on the board. Have the class brainstorm a list of contractions. Explain that a contraction is two words that are combined into one word. Also, explain that in a contraction the apostrophe is placed where the letters are removed from the original words. Write the words *have* and *not* on the board. Invite a volunteer to rewrite the word as a contraction and add the apostrophe in the correct location. Write on the board *This recipe requires these ingredients: sugar, lemon juice, flour, and baking soda.* Circle the colon in the sentence. Ask for volunteers to explain why the sentence has a colon. Write additional sentences on the board that also need a colon. Invite volunteers to add a colon and explain why it is needed.

A Capital Idea!

Divide the class into pairs, and give each pair a copy of the Capitalization and Punctuation Mini-Chart and a piece of paper. Have partners place their paper horizontally, draw nine columns, and label each column with a capitalization rule. Give each pair a section of newspaper and a highlighter. Ask students to select from their newspaper one page that includes very few advertisements. Have students read the text on the page and look for examples of each capitalization rule. Each time students find a rule, have them record the sentence under the appropriate heading on their paper and highlight the text in the newspaper. Invite pairs to trade papers with another pair of students. Have students review the new paper. Tell them to place a star next to each correct sentence. Collect student papers to check for understanding. To extend the activity, invite students to find additional sentences from other sources such as trade books, magazines, or novels. Remind students to only highlight the text on the newspaper.

Objective

Students will apply the rules of capitalization to a piece of writing.

Materials

- Capitalization and Punctuation Mini-Chart (page 82)
- blank paper
- newspaper
- highlighters

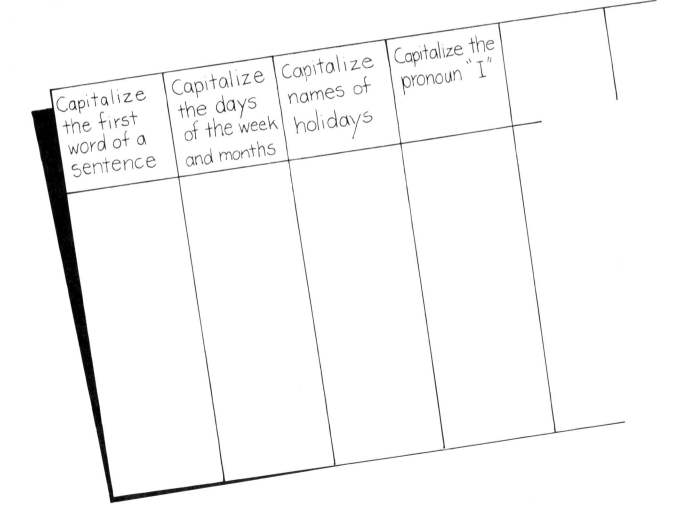

You Can Quote Me

Objective

Students will write and punctuate quotations correctly.

Materials

- chart paper
- reference materials

Divide the class into small groups. Give each group a piece of chart paper and a set of reference materials such as books of quotes, history books, or biographies. Have students use the reference materials to find quotations from famous people. Tell group members to list on their chart paper any quotes they find. Encourage group members to use correct punctuation and attribute the quote to the person who said it. For example, a group of students might write *"Give me liberty or give me death!" declared Patrick Henry* or *Thomas Paine remarked, "These are the times that try men's souls."* Remind students to use a more appropriate replacement for the worn-out word *said*. Display finished charts in the classroom, and have students review each chart to make sure correct punctuation was used.

Identify It

Objective

Students will use apostrophes to show possession and use colons to designate a list.

Materials

- construction paper
- magazines
- glue
- scissors

Divide the class into small groups. Give each group a piece of construction paper, a magazine, and glue. Tell students that each group will cut out pictures of related items. Tell groups to glue their pictures on their construction paper. Then, have them write at the bottom of their paper a sentence that shows who possesses the collection and what it is made of. Explain that students must use a colon and an apostrophe. For example, a group may write *Lisa, Tony, and Brett's collection of lipstick colors includes the following: cherry red, sunny orange, and smoky autumn.* Explain to the class that only Brett needs to have an apostrophe because the collection belongs to all three students. Have groups share their collection and read their sentence.

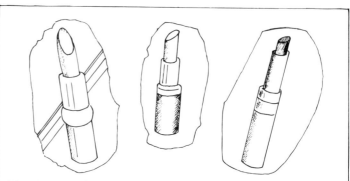

Lisa, Tony, and Brett's collection of lipstick colors includes the following: cherry red, sunny orange, and smoky autumn.

Using Capitalization

1. the highest points on the Earth are the mountains. _____

2. On may 20, 1980, Mount St. Helens erupted with great force. _____

3. By the following tuesday, the landscape looked _____
   completely different.

4. I read a book titled the forces of the earth. _____

5. This book explained how the grand tetons were formed. _____

6. These mountains are located in the state of wyoming. _____

7. My cousins eric and renee traveled there with us. _____

8. In the summer of 1998, i climbed to the top of Mount Whitney. _____

9. We met a volcanologist over the labor day weekend. _____

10. He told us, "the study of volcanoes is my life's work." _____

Using Commas

Use a comma between a city and a state.

St. Paul Minnesota

Use commas to separate a series of items.

We ate pie cake cookies and milk.

Use a comma in a date between the weekday and month.

Tuesday June 7

Use a comma in a date between the day and the year.

February 17 1997

Use a comma after a direct quotation.

"I see what you mean " said Mom.

Use a comma after the greeting in a friendly letter.

Dear Mr. Whitney

Use a comma after the closing in a letter.

Sincerely

Use commas to set aside an appositive

The soldier an army officer stood quietly.

Use a comma after an interjection.

Wow what a good deal.

Use a comma after a direct address.

Teresa could you come here?

Writing Makeovers • 5–6 © 2003 Creative Teaching Press

Using Apostrophes

Directions: Rewrite each set of words as a contraction. Make sure to add the apostrophe. Then, use the contraction correctly in a sentence.

1. let us   _____

_____

2. you are   _____

_____

3. we would   _____

_____

4. she will   _____

_____

5. they have   _____

_____

6. it is   _____

_____

7. who is   _____

_____

8. I am   _____

_____

Using Colons

Directions: Look at each list. Decide what kind of list it might be. Rewrite it as a sentence that uses a colon.

1. eggs

   butter

   milk

   cheese

_____

2. sweater

   gloves

   scarf

   warm socks

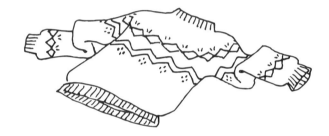

_____

3. igneous

   sedimentary

   metamorphic

_____

4. diamond

   ruby

   emerald

   sapphire

   topaz

_____

Writing Makeovers • 5–6 © 2003 Creative Teaching Press

Put It All Together

This section provides independent practice with the skills presented in the first seven sections. Students will experience editing for spelling, punctuation, and sentence structure, as well as evaluating word choices.

Getting Started

- **Review the Mini-Charts**
  Use the mini-charts to review the previously taught concepts. Invite students to review the word lists and tips before they complete the activities in this section.

Independent Learning

- **The Price of Vanity (page 92):** Point out that some of the misspelled words are homophones that are used incorrectly. Have students read each sentence carefully to be sure the correct homophone is used.
- **An Advertisement (page 93):** Tell students that if they locate the nouns first, it might be easier to locate adjectives that describe them afterwards.
- **Looking Out for Ducklings (page 94):** Remind students that they should replace overused adverbs and adjectives, but that they may need to reword the sentence.
- **A Science Discovery (page 95):** Remind students to watch carefully where quotation marks are used. Tell them to check that quotation marks appear at the beginning and end of a quote and that the first word of the quote is capitalized.

Wrap-Up

Have students write a biography about a family member. Remind students to include vivid verbs, descriptive nouns and adjectives, and proper punctuation. Invite students to trade completed papers with a classmate and proofread each other's paper. Encourage students to use the Editing Checklist (page 96) to carefully edit their writing for spelling, punctuation, sentence structure, and word choice.

The Price of Vanity

Directions: Read the story. Find the twelve misspelled words and draw an X over them. Write the word correctly over each misspelled word. Capitalize all proper nouns.

In a kingdom in a land long ago, there was a prince who was vary vain. prince junus felt he was the best-looking, the smartest, and the kindest person in all the kingdom of anglia. He was sure the peepol of the kingdom felt the same way. He wanted to here his citizens' compliments and praise. So prince junus disguised himself and traveld to the far reaches of anglia. In the market of bhopor, he found a sculptor selling statues. Among all the beutifuly carved objects, the prince saw a statue of the famous athlete hercules. "How much are you asking for this?" prince junus asked the sculptor. The sculptor replied, "I'll give you a good price. It is not one of my more popular peaces. You can have it for four pence." The prince laffed at the low prise. Then he saw a statue of his sister, princess kelta. "Oh, she is lovely," exclamed the prince. "How much for this one?" "That is a statue of princess kelta herself. I need to ask a little more for females," replied the sculptor. Then prince junus spied a statue of himself dressed in all his royal finery. His ego was suddenly inflated by the pride he felt viewing this likeness. He siad to the sculptor, "This is a fine image of the prince. This must have a very high value." "Well," replied the sculptor, "I am willing to make you a deal. If you pay me the prices I gave you for the other too, I will throw this won in for free."

Writing Makeovers • 5–6 © 2003 Creative Teaching Press

An Advertisement

Directions: Read the advertisement. Circle the 20 nouns. Underline the 14 adjectives. Capitalize words where appropriate.

Now Only $19.95!

Supermicro Radio

own the smallest radio in the world! This miniature wonder has the features of a regular radio, but it is so small it can easily fit in the palm of your hand. Supermicro Radio picks up shortwave bands as well as your favorite stations. This marvel is small enough to get lost in your pocket, but the sound it produces is not to be ignored. It features quality speakers, a station selector dial, and a telescoping antenna to bring in distant stations loud and clear. Don't miss out on this great deal! batteries not included.

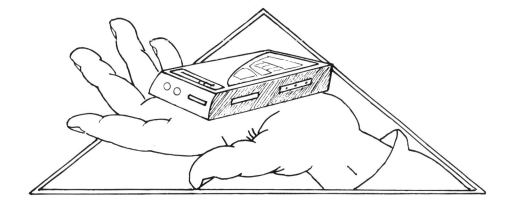

Looking Out for Ducklings

Directions: Read the story. Underline the six short sentences that could be combined with another sentence to make a more complex sentence. Circle the overused adverbs **very** and **suddenly.** Draw a box around the overused adjective **good.** Write a more appropriate word above each overused adverb and adjective. On another piece of paper, rewrite the story with all the corrections you made. Remember to combine the shorter sentences into longer sentences.

Jim stood in his front yard holding the hose. He was watering the newly planted daisies. He was watering the blooming roses. Suddenly, he heard a scrambling nearby. Jim looked to his right and suddenly he saw six baby ducks.

The ducklings had downy feathers in stripes and spots of black and yellow. These colors were good for camouflage. The ducklings were hard to see against the foliage. Jim noticed that their balance was not good. They'd tumble over the rough ground. They'd roll over each other.

The ducks didn't seem to notice him. He stood very still. He stood very quiet. The ducks would shuffle their little beaks into the soil. They were looking for bugs and other very tasty treats. Jim wondered, "Where's the mother? Usually she is nearby watching out for her babies."

Jim took a step toward the ducks. Suddenly, the mother duck came charging out of the bushes. She made a fair amount of noise and waddled straight toward Jim. "All right. I'll leave them alone," he called out to her. It seems she'd been watching all along. She was a good mother after all.

Writing Makeovers • 5–6 © 2003 Creative Teaching Press

A Science Discovery

Directions: Read the story. Circle the verbs. See if you can find all 42. Add any needed quotation marks, apostrophes, commas, and capital letters.

Melissa and John currently study plants in their science class. When they arrived on Monday, the materials for a new experiment were on their table. they set down their books and coats, and melissa quickly read the experiment card.

"Today you will observe the waste product of photosynthesis," read Melissa. "You will need the following materials: a small glass beaker a magnifying glass water and a fresh green leaf."

John answered, I ll gather all of the materials. you get the water." The two partners set about collecting their supplies.

John then remarked, "It says to fill the beaker with water. Then we submerge the leaf until it is fully covered with water." Melissa followed his instructions.

"Now we place it in a sunny location for an hour or until the container feels warm," instructed John. "We research our native plant report while we wait." They set the beaker in a sunny windowsill and began to work.

An hour later, John collected the beaker from the window. "look, Melissa!" he called out. "There are tiny bubbles on the leaf."

Melissa used a magnifying glass to examine the leaf. She observed little bubbles on the surface of the leaf. "Those are bubbles of oxygen released by the leaf. Oxygen is a waste product of photosynthesis. You can even see the little stomata on the bottom of the leaf! That is where carbon dioxide goes in and oxygen comes out."

Editing Checklist

The title of my writing is _____.

_____My sentences are complete and vary in

length and complexity.

_____I used a variety of sentence types.

_____I used descriptive nouns and capitalized proper nouns.

_____ I included appositives where appropriate.

_____I checked for overused verbs and replaced them with vivid verbs.

_____I included adjectives and adverbs that help give more details to the subjects and

actions of my writing.

_____I have used the correct homophones.

_____I checked my spelling and watched for frequently misspelled words.

_____I used proper punctuation.

Writing Makeovers • 5–6 © 2003 Creative Teaching Press